Addiction in the Lives
of Registered Nurses and
Their Wake-Up Jolt to Recovery

Addiction in the Lives of Registered Nurses and Their Wake-Up Jolt to Recovery

Carol Stanford

Hamilton Books

Lanham • Boulder • New York • Toronto • London

Published by Hamilton Books
An imprint of The Rowman & Littlefield Publishing Group, Inc.
4501 Forbes Boulevard, Suite 200, Lanham, Maryland 20706
Hamilton Books Acquisitions Department (301) 459-3366

Unit A, Whitacre Mews, 26-34 Stannary Street, London SE11 4AB

Library of Congress Control Number: 2018954707
ISBN 978-0-7618-7024-1 (pbk. : alk. cloth)
ISBN 978-0-7618-7049-4 (electronic)

∞™ The paper used in this publication meets the minimum requirements of American
National Standard for Information Sciences Permanence of Paper for Printed Library
Materials, ANSI/NISO Z39.48-1992.

Printed in the United States of America

To my loving husband, Michael, and daughter, Denisha, I thank God for you every day. You are two of the greatest blessings and gifts that He has given me.

To my late mother, Mildred A. Stewart, the most powerful, intelligent, loving woman I have ever known. Mom, thank you. Thank you for teaching me at an early age about the reality of Jesus Christ and sending me down a path of light and not of darkness. Thank you for many words of wisdom and the 26 years of my life you spent pouring wisdom, love, truth, and forgiveness into me. I had the most wonderful and loving experience growing up with a mom like you. I know at the appointed time, I will see you again in paradise.

Contents

List of Tables

Foreword

In *Addiction in the Lives of Registered Nurses and Their Wake-Up Jolt to Recovery*, through the real-life stories of registered nurses in recovery, Dr. Stanford brings to light the full range of experiences that health care professionals encounter when faced with a diagnosis of substance use disorder. During our ten years of working together, Dr. Stanford, in her role as the California Board of Registered Nursing's Diversion Program Manager, and I, as the Project Manager for the MAXIMUS Health Professional Diversion Program, witnessed well over 1,500 registered nurses face the stigma, challenges, defeats, and joys of a journey into recovery. While each individual's experience is their own, these narratives help us develop a larger understanding of the process of descent into addiction and growth in recovery. When engaged in a monitoring program, the nurses benefit from the support of their case managers, group facilitators and peers. They stock a toolbox of resources to manage the cravings, triggers, and challenges they experience with substance use disorder. But not without the denial and resistance that are hallmarks of this disease. These stories also reveal the vulnerabilities of most treatment or monitoring programs and the incredible drive the individuals encounter that pushes them to circumvent the structure and limits placed on them.

Her work with the nurses who placed their trust in her and exposed themselves and their experiences of recovery allowed Dr. Stanford to develop a theory regarding the five key factors that contribute to development of substance use disorder, and ways we can improve awareness and understanding of the disease as it impacts the nursing workforce.

Substance use disorder is a chronic, relapsing disease which is estimated to affect 14% of the general population. Health care professionals, especially nurses, are just as likely to fall prey to this vicious disorder as any other person. Nurses may be even more susceptible to it. The ready availability in the workplace of strong drugs, coupled with the tendency to overlook the power of their effects when handling them day to day, leads nurses to rationalize and diminish the risk of addiction. A consequence of the changes in laws regarding cannabis is the misperception that cannabis is harmless and is not addictive. Opioid use is at an all-time high in the U.S. Prescriptions for opioids are higher here than in any other country, and we are facing an Opioid Crisis. All of these dynamics have contributed to the problem and influenced the nurses who have shared their stories in this book.

There certainly is a stigma associated with this disease in the general public, but to health care professionals, it is also perceived as a weakness, a character flaw, and a disregard for the higher calling. With Dr. Stanford's gentle guidance, each of these nurses tells an account of shame, despair, and hardship, with eventual restoration to their true selves.

I encourage you to read this work with an open mind and an open heart. I express my appreciation to the nurses who allowed themselves to be vulnerable and who told their stories for this book. I send them love and healing as they continue on this journey. And I thank and honor Dr. Stanford, for having the sensitivity and compassion to help them bring their stories out into the light.

Virginia Matthews, RN, BSN, MBA
El Dorado Hills, California

Acknowledgments

I would first sincerely like to express my gratitude to my professor, Dr. Geller, for your patience, kindness, and continuous support throughout my research journey. Your guidance and encouragement, caring, friendship, and immense knowledge is more important to me than you can imagine.

To Dr. Chávez, thank you for your input as a professor who is knowledgeable about diversity and higher education. To Dr. Stringer, your expertise as a nurse practitioner and nurse manager were key in guiding me throughout this process. Thank you.

To Dr. Githens, you have been a major inspiration to me and your vast wisdom, knowledge, kindness, and continued support amaze me. Having you as a major professor in my education and training has made a difference in my personal and professional life. You have been a great mentor and I will be forever grateful! Thank you.

To my sister friends Christy, Liz, Marcella, and Stephanie: Wow, you are the best! We are forever connected. All I can say is God is good! To my other family members, friends, and others who have traveled with me on this journey: I want to say thank you.

To the participants in this study: you know who you are, you are the real "miracles" and champions of the day. The journeys you have traveled cannot be described merely on pen and paper. They are written in eternity. Thank you for trusting me and opening your lives to me like the flowers you represent. I appreciate you. You have a friend in me.

Editor: Meredith Linden has always appreciated other people's stories and worked with authors as a consultant and editor since 1994. After teaching for 14 years in the public education realm, she created her current business of Editorial Wizard. She assists writers with not only the written word, but also their personal obstacles to writing.

Acknowledgments

I

JOURNEY OF THE HIDDEN AND FOUNDATION OF MY INTEREST

"You are as close to a miracle as you are to a tragedy. I wanted to be a miracle and not a tragedy."

—Jasmine Jade

Chapter One

Introduction

Throughout history the nursing vocation has been identified as one of the most trusted professions of society. Year after year the public views nurses as the most honored and ethical professionals.[1] Yet, despite this or maybe because of it, nurses with substance use disorders are still hidden in the cloud of their profession. This book breaks through that cloud. It contains a study within that gives a voice to nurses who have experienced the devastating effects of substance use and abuse in their personal and professional lives. It explores the phenomenon of addiction in the lives of nurses who have directly experienced substance use disorders, but are now living in recovery. It is filled with the stories of nurses who talk about their personal experiences with substance use and abuse during various stages of their career. It discusses how these nurses have successfully dealt with addiction and what it took to find and maintain their recovery.

This book will provide greater insights and knowledge to the public and others within the healthcare community about their journey. The nurses also describe the systems of support within the healthcare setting that helped or hindered them from addressing their personal substance abuse issues. This information is important because substance use disorders in nursing have the potential to be more devastating than for other professions.[2] Nurses who are addicted place patients at risk, negatively impact the reputation of the facilities where they are employed, and frequently violate professional ethics.[3] Additionally, there are serious inadequacies within the nursing profession for identifying, intervening, and supporting nurses with substance use disorders, particularly nursing students. As you will see many nurses, including those included in the following narratives started having substance abuse problems in nursing school.

There are major discoveries from the narratives that will inform existing research. One of the first and most critical discoveries is the need for nurses to have a critical "wake-up-call" to jolt them from addiction to sobriety. This jolt is necessary to provide them with the clarity needed to embrace treatment and ultimately recovery. Additionally, the nurse's narratives underscore the impact recovery communities have on nurses who have major risks factors for substance abuse. This manuscript also includes recommendations outlined for educators, administrators, and other policymakers about increasing awareness, public safety, and training to identify and support nurses with substance use disorders.

NOTES

1. S. Horton-Deutsch, A. McNelis, and P. O'Haver Day, "Enhancing Mutual Accountability to Promote Quality, Safety, and Nurses' Recovery from Substance Use Disorders," *Archives of Psychiatric Nursing* 25 (2011).

2. D. Brooke, G. Edwards, and C. Taylor, "Addiction as an Occupational Hazard: 144 Doctors with Drug and Alcohol Problems," *British Journal of Addiction* 86 (1991).; M. Copp, "Drug Addiction," *RN* 72, no. 4 (2009); M. A. Naegle, "Drug and Alcohol Abuse in Nursing," *Nursing Life* 8, no. 1 (1988).; National Council of State Boards of Nursing (NCSBN), "Substance Use Disorder in Nursing, a Resource Manual and Guidelines for Alternative and Disciplinary Monitoring Programs," (2011), https://www.ncsbn.org/SUDN_11.pdf.

3. N. Darbro, "Alternative Diversion Programs for Nurses with Impaired Practice: Completers and Non-Completers," *Journal of Addictions Nursing* 16, no. 4 (2005); ibid.

BIBLIOGRAPHY

Brooke, D., G. Edwards, and C. Taylor. "Addiction as an Occupational Hazard: 144 Doctors with Drug and Alcohol Problems." *British Journal of Addiction* 86 (1991): 1011–16.

Copp, M. "Drug Addiction." *RN* 72, no. 4 (2009): 40–44.

Darbro, N. "Alternative Diversion Programs for Nurses with Impaired Practice: Completers and Non-Completers." *Journal of Addictions Nursing* 16, no. 4 (2005): 169–86.

Horton-Deutsch, S., A. McNelis, and P. O'Haver Day. "Enhancing Mutual Accountability to Promote Quality, Safety, and Nurses' Recovery from Substance Use Disorders." *Archives of Psychiatric Nursing* 25 (2011): 445.

Naegle, M. A. "Drug and Alcohol Abuse in Nursing." *Nursing Life* 8, no. 1 (1988): 42.54.

National Council of State Boards of Nursing (NCSBN). "Substance Use Disorder in Nursing, a Resource Manual and Guidelines for Alternative and Disciplinary Monitoring Programs." (2011): 280. https://www.ncsbn.org/SUDN_11.pdf.

Chapter Two

A Trusted Hidden Population

Although the nursing profession has been identified as one of the most virtuous and honorable professions in society,[1] studies have concluded that out of the estimated 2.8 million nurses currently working in the U.S., 10% to 20% (280,000 to 560,000) of those working in the nursing profession have experiences with substance use disorders.[2] There is a great illusion in society and among nurses themselves that they are immune to addiction. This is a serious issue, as nurses with substance use disorders are the most hidden population in society and place patients at risk.

Nurses with substance use and abuse issues themselves are fearful of being stigmatized by colleagues and managers; hence, many neither seek out nor receive treatment that would allow them to deal effectively with their problems.[3] There is a general lack of substance abuse knowledge within the nursing profession;[4] causing a deficiency in both the awareness to recognize and the competency to intervene and assist colleagues with substance abuse problems.[5] This is alarming because at some period in their career, either directly or indirectly, substance abuse affects all nurses.[6] A greater understanding of substance use disorders and a greater emphasis on the factors needed to confront the disease are needed. It is also important to understand that women make up approximately 91% of the nursing workforce,[7] and thus those with substance use disorders experience societal, ethical and sexual stigmatization and remain a hidden population.[8] Substance abuse incorporates many factors and is a complex phenomenon and cannot be explained by one simple theory. Recognizing this complexity, is an important aspect of understanding the information provided in this book and the stories of each of the nurses as they journeyed from addiction to recovery.

NOTES

1. A. M. Gallup, ed. *Gallup Poll: Public Opinion 2009* (Blue Ridge Summit, PA: Rowman & Littlefield Publishers, 2010).

2. D. Dunn, "Substance Abuse among Nurses – Intercession and Intervention," *Association of Operating Room Nurses Journal* 82, no. 2 (2005); S. A. Fogger and T. McGuinness, "Alabama's Nurse Monitoring Programs: The Nurse's Experience of Being Monitored," *Journal of Addictions Nursing* 20, no. 3 (2009); S. Horton-Deutsch, A. McNelis, and P. O'Haver Day, "Enhancing Mutual Accountability to Promote Quality, Safety, and Nurses' Recovery from Substance Use Disorders," *Archives of Psychiatric Nursing* 25 (2011); T. B. Monroe and H. Kenaga, "Don't Ask Don't Tell: Substance Abuse and Addiction among Nurses," *Journal of Clinical Nursing* 20 (2010); National Council of State Boards of Nursing (NCSBN), "Substance Use Disorder in Nursing, a Resource Manual and Guidelines for Alternative and Disciplinary Monitoring Programs," (2011), https://www.ncsbn.org/SUDN_11.pdf.; S. Ponech, "Signs," *Nursing Management* 31, no. 5 (2000); U.S. Department of Health and Human Services Health Resources and Services Administration. (HRSA), Preliminary Findings: 2013 National Sample Survey of Registered Nurses, (2013), http://bhpr.hrsa.gov/healthworkforce/reports/nursingworkforce/nursingworkforcefullreport.pdf.

3. T. F. Babor and R. M. Kadden, "Screening and Interventions for Alcohol and Drug Problems in Medical Settings: What Works? " *Journal of Trauma and Acute Care Surgery* 59, no. 3 (2005); A. H. Crisp et al., "Stigmatization of People with Mental Illness," *British Journal of Psychiatry* 177, no. 1 (2000); N. Darbro, "Alternative Diversion Programs for Nurses with Impaired Practice: Completers and Non-Completers," *Journal of Addictions Nursing* 16, no. 4 (2005); U. M. Fucito et al., "General Practitioners' Diagnostic Skills and Referral Practices in Managing Patients with Drug and Alcohol-Related Health Problems: Implications for Medical Training and Education Programs," *Drug and Alcohol Review* 22 (2003); P. Maher-Brisen, "Addiction: An Occupational Hazard in Nursing," *The American Journal of Nursing* 107, no. 8 (2007); A. T. McLellan and K. Meyers, "Contemporary Addiction Treatment: A Review of Systems Problems for Adults and Adolescents," *Biological Psychiatry* 56, no. 764–770 (2004); National Council of State Boards of Nursing (NCSBN), "Substance Use Disorder in Nursing, a Resource Manual and Guidelines for Alternative and Disciplinary Monitoring Programs;" R. Room, "Stigma, Social Inequality and Alcohol and Drug Use," *Drug Alcohol Review* 24 (2005).

4. T. B. Monroe, "Addressing Substance Misuse among Nursing Student: Development of a Prototype Alternative-to-Dismissal Policy," *Journal of Nursing Education* 8 (2009); D. Quinlan, "Impaired Nursing Practice: A National Perspective on Peer Assistance in the U.S.," *Journal of Addictions Nursing* 14, no. 149–155 (2003).

5. L. M. Pullen and L. A. Green, "Identification, Intervention and Education: Essential Curriculum Components for Chemical Dependency in Nurses," *The Journal of Continuing Education in Nursing* 28 (1997); Quinlan, "Impaired Nursing Practice: A National Perspective on Peer Assistance in the U.S.. ;" G. H. Rassool, "Curriculum Model, Course Development, and Evaluation of Substance Misuse Education for Health Care Professionals," ibid.15, no. 85–90 (2004).

6. D. Quinlan, "Impaired Nursing Practice: A National Perspective on Peer Assistance in the U.S.," ibid.14, no. 149–155 (2003).

7. U. S. Census Bureau, Men in Nursing Occupations: American Community Survey Highlight Report, (2013), https://www.census.gov/content/dam/Census/library/working-papers/2013/acs/2013_Landivar_02.pdf.

8. S. B. Blume, "Sexuality and Stigma: The Alcoholic Woman," *Alcohol Health and Research World* 15, no. 2 (1991); "Insights. Alcoholism in Women," *Harvard Mental Health Letter* 14, no. 9 (1998); S. B. Blume and M. L. Zilberman, *Addictive Disorders in Women. Clinical Textbook of Addictive Disorders*, 2 ed. (New York: Guilford Press, 1998); D. Goldberg, "Epidemiology of Mental Disorders in Primary Care Settings," *Epidemiologic reviews* 17, no. 1 (1995); S. C. Wilsnack, "Drinking, Sexuality, and Sexual Dysfunction in Women," *Alcohol Problems in Women* (1984); M. L. Zilberman et al., "Towards Best Practices in the

Treatment of Women with Addictive Disorders," *Addictive Disorders & Their Treatment* 1, no. 2 (2002).

BIBLIOGRAPHY

Babor, T. F., and R. M. Kadden. "Screening and Interventions for Alcohol and Drug Problems in Medical Settings: What Works? " *Journal of Trauma and Acute Care Surgery* 59, no. 3 (2005): S80–S87.

Blume, S. B. "Insights. Alcoholism in Women." *Harvard Mental Health Letter* 14, no. 9 (1998): 5-7.

———. "Sexuality and Stigma: The Alcoholic Woman." *Alcohol Health and Research World* 15, no. 2 (1991): 139.

Blume, S. B., and M. L. Zilberman. *Addictive Disorders in Women. Clinical Textbook of Addictive Disorders.* 2 ed. New York: Guilford Press, 1998.

Crisp, A. H., M. G. Gelder, S. Rix, H. I. Meltzer, and O. J. Rowlands. "Stigmatization of People with Mental Illness." *British Journal of Psychiatry* 177, no. 1 (2000): 4–7.

Darbro, N. "Alternative Diversion Programs for Nurses with Impaired Practice: Completers and Non-Completers." *Journal of Addictions Nursing* 16, no. 4 (2005): 169–86.

Dunn, D. "Substance Abuse among Nurses – Intercession and Intervention." *Association of Operating Room Nurses Journal* 82, no. 2 (2005): 87–88.

Fogger, S. A., and T. McGuinness. "Alabama's Nurse Monitoring Programs: The Nurse's Experience of Being Monitored." *Journal of Addictions Nursing* 20, no. 3 (2009): 142–49.

Fucito, U. M., B. S. Gomes, B. Murnion, and P. S. Haber. "General Practitioners' Diagnostic Skills and Referral Practices in Managing Patients with Drug and Alcohol-Related Health Problems: Implications for Medical Training and Education Programs." *Drug and Alcohol Review* 22 (2003): 417–24.

Gallup, A. M., ed. *Gallup Poll: Public Opinion 2009.* Blue Ridge Summit, PA: Rowman & Littlefield Publishers, 2010.

Goldberg, D. "Epidemiology of Mental Disorders in Primary Care Settings." *Epidemiologic reviews* 17, no. 1 (1995): 182–90.

Horton-Deutsch, S., A. McNelis, and P. O'Haver Day. "Enhancing Mutual Accountability to Promote Quality, Safety, and Nurses' Recovery from Substance Use Disorders." *Archives of Psychiatric Nursing* 25 (2011): 445.

Maher-Brisen, P. "Addiction: An Occupational Hazard in Nursing." *The American Journal of Nursing* 107, no. 8 (2007): 78–79.

McLellan, A. T., and K. Meyers. "Contemporary Addiction Treatment: A Review of Systems Problems for Adults and Adolescents." *Biological Psychiatry* 56, no. 764–770 (2004).

Monroe, T. B. "Addressing Substance Misuse among Nursing Student: Development of a Prototype Alternative-to-Dismissal Policy." *Journal of Nursing Education* 8 (2009): 272–77.

Monroe, T. B., and H. Kenaga. "Don't Ask Don't Tell: Substance Abuse and Addiction among Nurses." *Journal of Clinical Nursing* 20 (2010): 504–09.

National Council of State Boards of Nursing (NCSBN). "Substance Use Disorder in Nursing, a Resource Manual and Guidelines for Alternative and Disciplinary Monitoring Programs." (2011): 280. https://www.ncsbn.org/SUDN_11.pdf.

Ponech, S. "Signs." *Nursing Management* 31, no. 5 (2000): 32–38.

Pullen, L. M., and L. A. Green. "Identification, Intervention and Education: Essential Curriculum Components for Chemical Dependency in Nurses." *The Journal of Continuing Education in Nursing* 28 (1997): 211-16.

Quinlan, D. "Impaired Nursing Practice: A National Perspective on Peer Assistance in the U.S." *Journal of Addictions Nursing* 14, no. 149–155 (2003).

Rassool, G. H. "Curriculum Model, Course Development, and Evaluation of Substance Misuse Education for Health Care Professionals." *Journal of Addictions Nursing* 15, no. 85–90 (2004).

Room, R. "Stigma, Social Inequality and Alcohol and Drug Use." *Drug Alcohol Review* 24 (2005): 143–55.

U. S. Census Bureau. *Men in Nursing Occupations: American Community Survey Highlight Report.* 2013. https://www.census.gov/content/dam/Census/library/working-papers/2013/acs/2013_Landivar_02.pdf.

U.S. Department of Health and Human Services Health Resources and Services Administration. (HRSA). *Preliminary Findings: 2013 National Sample Survey of Registered Nurses.* 2013. http://bhpr.hrsa.gov/healthworkforce/reports/nursingworkforce/nursingworkforcefull-report.pdf.

Wilsnack, S. C. "Drinking, Sexuality, and Sexual Dysfunction in Women." *Alcohol Problems in Women* (1984): 189–227.

Zilberman, M. L., H. Tavares, S. B. Blume, and N. el-Guebaly. "Towards Best Practices in the Treatment of Women with Addictive Disorders." *Addictive Disorders & Their Treatment* 1, no. 2 (2002): 39–46.

Chapter Three

Personal Stance and Beliefs

My interest in this topic developed through my own life experiences. I voluntarily worked with the mentally ill as a teenager, as well as majored in social work for my undergraduate studies. I have always had a heart for social and public issues. Drawing on my social services orientation, a calling has drawn me to engage with nurses suffering from alcohol and substance abuse. It became a path that was part of a larger intention for me. Senge, Scharmer, Jaworski, and Flowers[1] suggested, "When our work is informed by a larger intention, it's infused with who we are and our purpose in being alive."

Explorations and research usually emerge from beliefs, issues, conflicts, or concerns that have happened in daily work and life.[2] Alcoholism has had a major impact on my life. I lost two half-brothers to alcoholism and have a brother in and out of hospitals struggling with alcohol addiction issues. Additionally, I have had friends and loved ones who have also dealt with issues of alcohol and drug abuse. Because of these personal experiences, I became acutely aware of how substance use disorders plague the human condition.

My professional experiences working for the State of California also informed my interest. For more than 22 years, I worked first as a Program Analyst and later as Program Manager for the California Board of Registered Nursing's (BRN) Intervention Program (formerly known as the "Diversion Program"). The BRN Intervention Program is a comprehensive chemical dependency monitoring program. In this role, I had numerous experiences working with nurses and other health professionals who were suffering from substance use disorders and working to overcome the disease. I became acutely aware of the reality of the needs of nurses within the profession and their lack of understanding surrounding their own vulnerabilities and risks. I clearly understood the influencing power licensing agencies have in being a major tool to guide nurses into sobriety and recovery when a nurse's substance use disorder is discovered and handled appropriately. These experiences provide a foundation for my interest.

Thus, I am fully cognizant that I have assumptions that developed from my own life experiences and tacit career experiences, which include believing that (a) addiction in any form, especially as it relates to substance use and abuse, is a phenomenon that is complex and dangerous and (b) nurses with substance use disorders endanger themselves and the public. Additionally, (c) I believe nurses within the profession are neither receiving sufficient education nor support early enough in their careers regarding their own personal risks for a substance use disorder and (d) more information needs to be provided regarding the availability of treatment. Finally, (e) I approached the narrative study contained in this manuscript believing that nurses can have a successful career while in recovery from substance abuse.

LIMITATIONS WITHIN THIS MANUSCRIPT

The methodology used within this manuscript was narrative inquiry. This type of research is understood to be research that is not necessarily transferable. I am aware that the nurses who participated were specific samples of individuals and that there are limits to their generalization to the larger population. I sought through this study to offer an in-depth look at the experiences and challenges of a small number of nurses living in recovery from substance use disorders hoping their stories would inform and add to the understanding of the phenomenon of recovery from substance abuse within the nurse profession. It drew on a small region in California and may not be generalized to the experiences of nurses in other locations.

The study also dealt with a particular time frame related to the nurses. Furthermore, since this was a narrative study that was dependent upon self-disclosure, the long history of stigmatism of substance abuse in the nursing profession may have been an impediment to nurses wholeheartedly coming forward with information regarding their substance abuse.

The study sought to provide insight into nurses' lived experiences with recovery. It sought to understand the available support for recovery provided by the profession. This study seeks to be meaningful for nurse educators and nurses in general. It hopes to provide insights for early career nurses in understanding their own individual risks for substance abuse. The findings of this study have added to the body of knowledge that exists regarding nurses with substance use disorders and may corroborate prior research on aspects of substance abuse in the nursing profession. It seeks to add to the conversation surrounding the need for greater preparation and support of nurses with substance use disorders.

DEFINITION OF TERMS

In order to have a consensus of how specific terms are used throughout this book, the following definition of general terms are listed below:

Addiction

A primary, chronic relapsing complex brain disease that is categorized by habitual drug seeking and use, despite destructive consequences. A disease that changes areas of the brain that are "critical to judgment, decision-making, learning and memory, and behavior control."[3]

Chemical Dependency

Also labeled "substance use disorder"—"a medical disorder in which an individual experiences a compulsion to take a drug either continuously or periodically, in order to experience its psychic effects or to avoid the discomfort of its absence."[4]

Nurse

This term is used relating only to registered nurses (RN) who are practitioners, who have passed the appropriate nursing licensing requirements, and have fulfilled the required educational requirements determined by each jurisdiction or state.[5]

Recovery

The process of change through which one makes improved health choices, strives for health and wellness, and endeavors to reach one's full potential. It is a process that involves abstaining from unlawful drugs, nonprescription medication, and alcohol use if one is addicted.[6]

Substance Abuse

"A maladaptive pattern of alcohol or other drug use, including medications, leading to functional problems for the individual who uses."[7]

Substance Use Disorders

"State of dependency on mind-altering chemicals with continuing use that persists despite negative consequences."[8] Combines the DSM-IV categories of substance abuse and substance dependence into a single disorder measured on a continuum from mild to severe.[9]

Treatment

"Formalized and structured" management for persons with a substance use disorder "consisting of group therapy, individual therapy, and education. Goals are directed toward individuals gaining skills needed to obtain and maintain abstinence from drug use."[10]

NOTES

1. P. M. Senge et al., *Presence: An Exploration of Profound Change in People, Organizations, and Society* (New York: Crown Business, 2005)., 140.
2. Ibid.
3. National Institute on Drug Abuse (NIDA), Drug Abuse and Addiction: The Basics, (2016), http://www.drugabuse.gov/publications/media-guide/science-drug-abuse-addiction-basics., 4.
4. National Council of State Boards of Nursing (NCSBN), "Substance Use Disorder in Nursing, a Resource Manual and Guidelines for Alternative and Disciplinary Monitoring Programs," (2011), https://www.ncsbn.org/SUDN_11.pdf., 236.
5. S. K. Comer, "Nursing Licensure, Legislation and Nurse Practice Acts," Adventure of the American Mind—Governors State University, http://aam.govst.edu/projects/scomer/student_page1.html.
6. Substance Abuse and Mental Health Services Administration (SAMHSA), Recovery and Recovery Support, (2015), http://www.samhsa.gov/recovery.
7. American Psychiatric Association (APA), *Diagnostic and Statistical Manual of Mental Disorders*, 4 ed., Dsm-Iv-Tr (Arlington, VA: American Psychiatric Association, 2000)., 7.
8. National Council of State Boards of Nursing (NCSBN), "Substance Use Disorder in Nursing, a Resource Manual and Guidelines for Alternative and Disciplinary Monitoring Programs," 239.
9. American Psychiatric Association (APA), *Diagnostic and Statistical Manual of Mental Disorders*, Dsm-5 (Arlington, VA: American Psychiatric Association, 2013).
10. National Council of State Boards of Nursing (NCSBN), "Substance Use Disorder in Nursing, a Resource Manual and Guidelines for Alternative and Disciplinary Monitoring Programs.," 236.

BIBLIOGRAPHY

American Psychiatric Association (APA). *Diagnostic and Statistical Manual of Mental Disorders.* Dsm-5. Arlington, VA: American Psychiatric Association, 2013.
———. *Diagnostic and Statistical Manual of Mental Disorders.* Dsm-Iv-Tr. 4 ed. Arlington, VA: American Psychiatric Association, 2000.
Comer, S. K. "Nursing Licensure, Legislation and Nurse Practice Acts." Adventure of the American Mind–Governors State University, http://aam.govst.edu/projects/scomer/student_page1.html.
National Council of State Boards of Nursing (NCSBN). "Substance Use Disorder in Nursing, a Resource Manual and Guidelines for Alternative and Disciplinary Monitoring Programs." (2011): 280.https://www.ncsbn.org/SUDN_11.pdf.
National Institute on Drug Abuse (NIDA). *Drug Abuse and Addiction: The Basics.* 2016. http://www.drugabuse.gov/publications/media-guide/science-drug-abuse-addiction-basics.
Senge, P. M., C. O. Scharmer, J. Jaworski, and B. S. Flowers. *Presence: An Exploration of Profound Change in People, Organizations, and Society.* New York: Crown Business, 2005.
Substance Abuse and Mental Health Services Administration (SAMHSA). *Recovery and Recovery Support.* 2015. http://www.samhsa.gov/recovery.

II

ADDICTION AND HEALTHCARE

"It's only one life to live . . . very often substance abuse is self-medication. And it helps one get through life to a certain extent until it turns on oneself."

—Napeta

Chapter Four

History of Substance Abuse and the Healthcare Professional

Substance abuse continues to be prevalent within the general public. Approximately 8.1% of adults, or 21.5 million people in America, have a substance use disorder with an additional 3.3% having both co-occurring mental illness and substance use disorder.[1] Extensive research exists surrounding the treatment of substance use disorders and recovery in the general population; however, less is known about substance use disorders and recovery in the nursing profession. To provide an important foundation the following chapters will provide a short overview of the history of substance abuse for the health professional, how substance abuse impacts the nursing profession and what is known generally regarding recovery.

Throughout the history of the healthcare profession, drug addiction has been cited as a concerning issue for medical personnel. Just as substance use disorder is a disease that afflicts the public, this disease also impacts physicians, nurses, dentists, and other healthcare workers.[2] Complex and stressful working conditions, along with easy access to substances, have contributed to this.[3] Research has suggested that some healthcare professionals sought relief from pain and rationalized illegal drug use, creating a gateway to substance use disorders.[4] Since nurses make up the largest group of professionals in healthcare, when issues develop involving substance use and abuse, nurses are more visible and usually more stigmatized.[5] Substance abuse is of specific concern for nurses since they are responsible for the intimate care and well-being of patients and can cause harm.[6]

Chapter 4

ADDICTION AND SUBSTANCE USE DISORDERS IN THE 1800S AND EARLY 1900S

As early as 1869, the substance abuse problem of physicians was noted.[7] In the 1900s, the medical profession was dominated by males and it was the primary profession that experienced the most substance abuse; although the percentage of physicians affected was in question.[8] Dr. D.T. Crothers described in a paper he presented to the New York Medical Association in the late 1800s that 21% of his physician patients were abusing alcohol or drugs.[9] Additionally, in a personal study of 3,244 physicians, Crothers noted that anywhere from 6-10% reported a substance use disorder.[10]

Throughout early history, two well-known physicians were cited as examples of the impact of substance abuse within the medical profession. Both William Halsted, a well-known professor and surgeon at Johns Hopkins, and the renowned neurologist and professor Sigmund Freud have documented histories involving substance abuse.[11]

In the late 19th and early 20th centuries, there were many treatment institutions known as "addiction cure franchises" which were established after the American Association of the Cure of the Inebriety was founded in 1870.[12] However, as time progressed, attitudes towards individuals with substance use disorders during the early 1920s and 1930s became hardened. Healthcare professionals viewed "addiction" as a "manifestation of psychopathy" or "form of twisted personality."[13] The view of seeing "addicts" as "fiends"[14] that were "useless" or "dangerous" and "amoral or immoral beings"[15] led to increasing stigmatism surrounding drug addiction. During this period, drug addiction treatment in America ceased.[16] It took over 50 years for specialized treatment and a national system related to addiction and drug use to be reestablished. The treatment of substance use disorders needed to evolve along with the "recognition of addiction medicine as a legitimate medical specialty."[17]

FROM ADDICTION TO SUBSTANCE USE DISORDERS

According to the National Epidemiologic Survey on Alcohol and Related Conditions (NESARC), drug dependence and abuse are widespread and are greatly disabling conditions that often go untreated.[18] The American Medical Association (AMA) acknowledged alcoholism as a disease in 1956, and all other forms of substance abuse were designated as a disease in 1987. The AMA recognized that healthcare professionals were not receiving the same treatment opportunities as the general public.[19] The AMA, along with the American Nurses Association (ANA), subsequently pushed through legislation for every state to develop non-public peer assistance intended to assist physicians and nurses with substance use issues.

While many research studies have used the term "addiction" to describe substance abuse and chemical dependency, the accepted clinical term now being used is "substance use disorder." The term *substance use disorder* is a medical term and is the most "current and accepted terminology used by the American Psychiatric Association (APA)."[20] It is defined as a "compulsive physical or psychological urge to use chemicals (drugs and/or alcohol) and the inability to stop using them despite all the problems caused by their use."[21] In *The Diagnostic and Statistical Manual-V* (*DSM-V*), the APA "replaced categories of substance abuse and substance dependence with a single category: substance use disorder."[22] This definition is now presently being used to replace all other words or terms such as habituation, addiction, excessive drinking, alcoholism and other older words for people who use or abuse mind-altering substances.[23]

PRESCRIPTION DRUG ABUSE, AMERICA'S EPIDEMIC

More research on substance abuse, as it related to physicians, began to appear in the literature of the early 20th century.[24] This literature began to outline how prescription drug abuse impacted physicians and other healthcare professionals. Prescription drug abuse became an epidemic in America and is currently a major health concern.[25] The most recent CDC report[26] noted that more people died in 2014 from drug overdoses than in any other year with the majority of those deaths the result of pain relieving prescription opioids.

Research suggests that health care professionals have been particularly impacted by substance abuse related to prescription drugs.[27] The availability of drugs and increased opportunities for healthcare professionals to divert drugs leaves them particularly vulnerable to prescription drug misuse. In a study of 55 physicians, with 94.5% of the subjects self-identified as male, 69.1% reported a "lifetime misuse of prescriptions."[28]

SUBSTANCE ABUSE AS AN OCCUPATIONAL HAZARD

Members of all related health professions, in particular nurses, physicians, pharmacists, and dentists are known to have the greatest struggle with substance use disorders. Additionally, in the healthcare industry, different specialties within the healthcare profession have higher levels of the prevalence of substance abuse than others.[29] Specific specialties among physicians— such as psychiatrists, emergency medicine physicians, anesthesiologists, and family practitioners—and among nurses—such as nurse anesthetists, critical care, and emergency room nurses—have the highest rates of substance abuse.[30] The consequences of substance use disorders affect those in medical field occupations through increased absenteeism, a demoralized workforce, mistakes with patients, employee injuries, and theft of drugs and resources.[31]

Pharmacists' risks of substance abuse have not been widely researched.[32] In a study of 32 pharmacists with substance use disorders several risk indicators were identified: including easy access to drugs, a stressful work environment, a culture that accepts diversion of medication, barriers to substance abuse treatment, and a lack of education about substance use disorders.[33] These are the same risk factors as experienced by physicians.[34] One pharmacist participant indicated there is an unlimited source with no checks, "basically, it was available. I mean, we're in a position where there's a lot of things that are accessible. Like, if you're a bartender, you might get a sip of liquor for free. It's accessibility."[35] Similarly, dentists have a prevalence of abuse that has been found to mirror that of the general public or may be higher due to their easy access to drugs.[36]

The NESARC study concluded that to assist those medical professionals with substance abuse issues, there should be immediate action taken to educate healthcare professionals, the public, and policymakers about substance use disorders and their treatment.[37] The Obama administration, in response to the prescription drug abuse epidemic, released a wide-ranging action strategy to counter the substance abuse crisis.[38] This action plan addressed four areas needed to help decrease prescription drug abuse: education, monitoring, enforcement, and appropriate disposal of narcotics.[39] It is recommended that programs be developed to reduce personal suffering, stigma, and the adverse societal impact of substance use disorders.[40]

NOTES

1. S. L. Hedden, "Behavioral Health Trends in the United States: Results from the 2014 National Survey on Drug Use and Health," (2015), http://www.samhsa.gov/data/sites/default/files/NSDUH-FRR1-2014/NSDUH-FRR1-2014.pdf

2. G. A. Kenna and M. D. Wood, "Substance Use by Pharmacy and Nursing Practitioners and Students in a Northeastern State," American Journal of Health-System Pharmacy 61, no. 9 (2004); J. I. Rojas et al., "Substance Abuse Patterns and Psychiatric Symptomology among Health Care Professionals and Non–Health Care Professionals Evaluated in an Outpatient Program for Impaired Professionals," Addictive Disorders & Their Treatment 13, no. 2 (2014).

3. T. Mullaney, "Survey: Nurses under Dangerous Stress," McKnight's Long-Term Care News 35, no. 8 (2014); A. M. Trinkoff and C. L. Storr, "Work Schedule Characteristics and Substance Use in Nurses," American Journal of Industrial Medicine 34 (1998b); A. P. Wolfgang, "Job Stress in the Health Professions. A Study of Physicians, Nurses and Pharmacists," Behavioral Medicine 14, no. 1 (1988).

4. B. Heise, "The Historical Context of Addiction in the Nursing Profession: 1850-1982," Journal of Addictions Nurse 14, no. 3 (2003); B. W. Lex, "Alcohol and Other Drug Abuse among Women," Alcohol Research and Health 18 (1994); N. R. Stepter, "Drug Abuse among Nurses," Nursing Management 13, no. 12 (1982).

5. U.S. Department of Health and Human Services Health Resources and Services Administration. (HRSA), Preliminary Findings: 2013 National Sample Survey of Registered Nurses, (2013), http://bhpr.hrsa.gov/healthworkforce/reports/nursingworkforce/nursingworkforcefull-report.pdf.; M. F. Shaw et al., "Physicians and Nurses with Substance Use Disorders," Journal of Advanced Nursing 47 (2004).

6. Rojas et al., "Substance Abuse Patterns and Psychiatric Symptomology among Health Care Professionals and Non–Health Care Professionals Evaluated in an Outpatient Program for Impaired Professionals."

7. J. Paget, "What Becomes of Medical Students," St. Bartholomew's Hospital Report 5 (1869).

8. D. T. Courtwright, Dark Paradise: A History of Opiate Addiction in America (Cambridge, MA: Harvard University Press, 2009), 41.

9. as cited in G. M. Gould and J. H. Lloyd, *The Philadelphia Medical Journal, 4* (Philadelphia, PA: Philadelphia Medical Publishing Company, 1899), 835–36.

10. As cited in ibid., 836.

11. Courtwright, Dark Paradise: A History of Opiate Addiction in America; H. Markel, An Anatomy of Addiction: Sigmund Freud, William Halsted and the Miracle Drug, Cocaine (New York: Pantheon Books, 2012).

12. W. L. White, "The Role of Recovering Physicians in 19th Century Addiction Medicine: An Organizational Case Study," Journal of Addictive Diseases 19, no. 2 (2000).

13. Courtwright, Dark Paradise: A History of Opiate Addiction in America, 3.

14. M. I. Wilbert, "The Number and Kind of Drug Addicts," Public Health Reports (1896-1970) 30 (1915): 2290.

15. M. Singer and J. B. Page, The Social Value of Drug Addicts: The Uses of the Useless (Walnut Creek, CA: Left Coast Press, 2013), 17.

16. White, "The Role of Recovering Physicians in 19th Century Addiction Medicine: An Organizational Case Study."

17. Ibid., 7.

18. W. M. Compton et al., "Substance Dependence and Other Psychiatric Disorders among Drug Dependent Subjects: Race and Gender Correlates," American Journal of Addiction 9 (2000).

19. National Council of State Boards of Nursing (NCSBN), "Substance Use Disorder in Nursing, a Resource Manual and Guidelines for Alternative and Disciplinary Monitoring Programs," (2011), https://www.ncsbn.org/SUDN_11.pdf.

20. American Psychiatric Association (APA), Diagnostic and Statistical Manual of Mental Disorders, 4 ed., Dsm-Iv-Tr (Arlington, VA: American Psychiatric Association, 2000), 7.

21. Ibid.

22. National Institute on Drug Abuse (NIDA), Drug Abuse and Addiction: The Basics, (2016), http://www.drugabuse.gov/publications/media-guide/science-drug-abuse-addiction-basics. 1.

23. J. Morrison, Dsm-5® Made Easy: The Clinician's Guide to Diagnosis (New York: The Guilford Press, 2014).

24. S. Harris, "Alcoholism and Drug Addiction among Physicians of Alabama," Transcripts Medical Association of Alabama (1914).

25. Centers for Disease Control and Prevention (CDC), "Vital Signs: Overdoses of Prescription Opioid Pain Relievers-United States 1999-2008," MMWR 60 (2011), http://www.cdc.gov/homeandrecreationalsafety/rxbrief/index.html

26. As cited in D. Dowell, T. M. Haegerich, and R. Chou, "Cdc Guideline for Prescribing Opioids for Chronic Pain–United States, 2016mmwr Recommended Report," 65 RR-1, no. 1–49 (2016).

27. M. E. Brown et al., "Impairment Issues for Healthcare Professionals: Review and Recommendations," Substance Abuse 23, no. S1 (2002); D. Joranson et al., "Trends in Medical Use and Abuse of Opioid Analgesics," Journal of American Medical Association 283 (2000); Rojas et al., "Substance Abuse Patterns and Psychiatric Symptomology among Health Care Professionals and Non–Health Care Professionals Evaluated in an Outpatient Program for

Impaired Professionals."; Trinkoff and Storr, "Work Schedule Characteristics and Substance Use in Nurses."

28. L. J. Merlo, S. M. Cummings, and L. B. Cottler, "Recovering Substance-Impaired Pharmacists' Views Regarding Occupational Risks for Addiction," Journal of the American Pharmacists Association 22, no. 6 (2012): 3.

29. L. Blazer and P. Mansfield, "A Comparison of Substance Use Rates among Female Nurses, Clerical Workers and Blue-Collar Workers," Journal of Advanced Nursing 21, no. 2 (1995); T. L. Hughes, M. Howard, and D. Henry, "Comparison of Alcohol and Drug Use by Nurses and Other Occupational Groups," Substance Use and Misuse 37, no. 11 (2002); J. Rose, M. Campbell, and G. Skipper, "Prognosis for Emergency Physician with Substance Abuse Recovery: 5-Year Outcome Study," Western Journal of Emergency Medicine 15, no. 1 (2014); G. E. Skipper, M. D. Campbell, and R. L. Dupont, "Anesthesiologists with Substance Use Disorders: A 5-Year Outcome Study from 16 State Physician Health Programsanesthesia Analgesi," 109, no. 891–896 (2009).

30. P. H. Hughes et al., "Physician Substance Use by Medical Specialtyjournal of Addictive Diseases," 18 2, no. 23–37 (1999); M. A. Naegle, "Drug and Alcohol Abuse in Nursing," Nursing Life 8, no. 1 (1988); "Mental Health and Substance-Related Health Care," in Addictions and Substance Abuse: Strategies for Advanced Nursing Practice, ed. M. Naegle and C. E. D'Avanzo (Saddle River, NJ: Prentice Hall Health, 2001); Substance Abuse and Addiction among Registered Nurses 2ed. (New York: Springer Publishing Company, 2006); A. M. Trinkoff and C. L. Storr, "Substance Use among Nurses: Differences between Specialties," American Journal of Public Health 88 (1998a).

31. C. J. Cherpitel, "Alcohol and Injuries: A Review of International Emergency Room Studies since 1995," Drug and Alcohol Review 26 (2007); R. B. Coambs and M. P. McAndrews, "The Effects of Psychoactive Substances on Workplace Performance," in Drug Testing in the Workplace, ed. S. Macdonald and P. M. Roman, Research Advances in Alcohol and Drug Problems (Boston, MA: Springer, 1994); S. Cohen, "Drugs in the Workplace," Journal of Clinical Psychiatry 45 (1984); M. R. Frone, "Alcohol, Drugs, and Workplace Safety Outcomes: A View from a General Model of Employee Substance Use and Productivity," in The Psychology of Workplace Safety ed. J. Barling and M. R. Frone (Washington, DC: American Psychological Association, 2004); "Employee Alcohol and Illicit Drug Use: Scope, Causes and Organizational Consequences," in Handbook of Organizational Behavior, ed. C. L. Cooper and J. Barling (Thousand Oaks, CA: Sage Publications, 2009); S. W. Gust et al., eds., Drugs in the Workplace: Research and Evaluation Data Nida Research Monograph No. 100 (Rockville, MD: U.S. Department of Health & Human Services, 1990); J. K. Martin, J. M. Kraft, and P. M. Roman, "Extent and Impact of Alcohol and Drug Use Problems in the Workplace: A Review of the Empirical Evidence," in Drug Testing in the Workplace, ed. S. Macdonald and P. M. Roman (New York: Plenum Press, 1994); J. Rehm, B. Taylor, and Room. R., "Global Burden of Disease from Alcohol, Illicit Drugs and Tobacco," Drug and Alcohol Review 25 (2006); R. Room, "Stigma, Social Inequality and Alcohol and Drug Use," Drug Alcohol Review 24 (2005); R. S. Spicer, T. R. Miller, and G. S. Smith, "Worker Substance Use Workplace Problems and the Risk of Occupational Injury: A Matched Case-Control Study," Quarterly Journal of Studies on Alcohol 64 (2003).

32. Merlo, Cummings, and Cottler, "Recovering Substance-Impaired Pharmacists' Views Regarding Occupational Risks for Addiction."

33. Ibid.

34. R. H. Coombs, Drug-Impaired Professionals (Cambridge, MA: Harvard University Press, 1997); Courtwright, Dark Paradise: A History of Opiate Addiction in America.

35. Merlo, Cummings, and Cottler, "Recovering Substance-Impaired Pharmacists' Views Regarding Occupational Risks for Addiction," 483.

36. J. C. Marnewick and A. W. Van Zyl, "Substance Abuse among Oral Healthcare Workers," South African Dental Journal 69, no. 4 (2014).

37. As cited in W. M. Compton et al., "Prevalence, Correlates, Disability, and Comorbidity of Dsm-Iv Drug Abuse and Dependence in the United States: Results from the National Epidemiologic Survey on Alcohol and Related Conditions," Archives of general psychiatry 64 (2007).

38. R. C. Denisco et al., "Prevention of Prescription Opioid Abuse the Role of the Dentist," The Journal of the American Dental Association 142 (2011); White House, "Epidemic: Responding to America's Prescription Drug Abuse Crisis," (Washington, DC: Office of the National Drug Control Policy, 2011).
39. Denisco et al., "Prevention of Prescription Opioid Abuse the Role of the Dentist."
40. Compton et al., "Substance Dependence and Other Psychiatric Disorders among Drug Dependent Subjects: Race and Gender Correlates."

BIBLIOGRAPHY

American Psychiatric Association (APA). *Diagnostic and Statistical Manual of Mental Disorders.* Dsm-Iv-Tr. 4 ed. Arlington, VA: American Psychiatric Association, 2000.

Blazer, L., and P. Mansfield. "A Comparison of Substance Use Rates among Female Nurses, Clerical Workers and Blue-Collar Workers." *Journal of Advanced Nursing* 21, no. 2 (1995): 305–13.

Brown, M. E., A. M. Trinkoff, A. G. Christen, and E. J. Dole. "Impairment Issues for Healthcare Professionals: Review and Recommendations." *Substance Abuse* 23, no. S1 (2002): 155–65.

Centers for Disease Control and Prevention (CDC). "Vital Signs: Overdoses of Prescription Opioid Pain Relievers-United States 1999-2008." *MMWR* 60(2011): 1487–92. Published electronically 2011. http://www.cdc.gov/homeandrecreationalsafety/rxbrief/index.html

Cherpitel, C. J. "Alcohol and Injuries: A Review of International Emergency Room Studies since 1995." *Drug and Alcohol Review* 26 (2007): 201–14.

Coambs, R. B., and M. P. McAndrews. "The Effects of Psychoactive Substances on Workplace Performance." In *Drug Testing in the Workplace*, edited by S. Macdonald and P. M. Roman. Research Advances in Alcohol and Drug Problems, 77–102. Boston, MA: Springer, 1994.

Cohen, S. "Drugs in the Workplace." *Journal of Clinical Psychiatry* 45 (1984): 4–8.

Compton, W. M., L. B. Cottler, A. B. Abdallah, D. L. Phelps, E. L. Spitznagel, and J. C. Horton. "Substance Dependence and Other Psychiatric Disorders among Drug Dependent Subjects: Race and Gender Correlates." *American Journal of Addiction* 9 (2000): 113–25.

Compton, W. M., Y. F. Thomas, F. S. Stinson, and B. F. Grant. "Prevalence, Correlates, Disability, and Comorbidity of Dsm-Iv Drug Abuse and Dependence in the United States: Results from the National Epidemiologic Survey on Alcohol and Related Conditions." *Archives of general psychiatry* 64 (2007): 566–76.

Coombs, R. H. *Drug-Impaired Professionals.* Cambridge, MA: Harvard University Press, 1997.

Courtwright, D. T. *Dark Paradise: A History of Opiate Addiction in America.* Cambridge, MA: Harvard University Press, 2009.

Denisco, R. C., G. A. Kenna, M. G. O'Neil, R. J. Kulich, P. A. Moore, W. T. Kane, and N. P. Katz. "Prevention of Prescription Opioid Abuse the Role of the Dentist." *The Journal of the American Dental Association* 142 (2011): 800.

Dowell, D., T. M. Haegerich, and R. Chou. "Cdc Guideline for Prescribing Opioids for Chronic Pain–United States, 2016mmwr Recommended Report." *65* RR-1, no. 1–49 (2016).

Frone, M. R. "Alcohol, Drugs, and Workplace Safety Outcomes: A View from a General Model of Employee Substance Use and Productivity." In *The Psychology of Workplace Safety* edited by J. Barling and M. R. Frone, 127-56. Washington, DC: American Psychological Association, 2004.

———. "Employee Alcohol and Illicit Drug Use: Scope, Causes and Organizational Consequences." In *Handbook of Organizational Behavior*, edited by C. L. Cooper and J. Barling. Thousand Oaks, CA: Sage Publications, 2009.

Gould, G. M., and J. H. Lloyd. *The Philadelphia Medical Journal, 4.* Philadelphia, PA: Philadelphia Medical Publishing Company, 1899.

Gust, S. W., J. M. Walsh, L. B. Thomas, and D. J. Crouch, eds. *Drugs in the Workplace: Research and Evaluation Data* Nida Research Monograph No. 100. Rockville, MD: U.S. Department of Health & Human Services, 1990.

Harris, S. "Alcoholism and Drug Addiction among Physicians of Alabama." *Transcripts Medical Association of Alabama* (1914): 685–91.

Hedden, S. L. "Behavioral Health Trends in the United States: Results from the 2014 National Survey on Drug Use and Health." (2015). http://www.samhsa.gov/data/sites/default/files/NSDUH-FRR1-2014/NSDUH-FRR1-2014.pdf

Heise, B. "The Historical Context of Addiction in the Nursing Profession: 1850-1982." *Journal of Addictions Nurse* 14, no. 3 (2003): 117–24.

Hughes, P. H., C. L. Storr, N. A. Brandenburg, D. C. Baldwin, J. C. Anthony, and D. V. Sheehan. "Physician Substance Use by Medical Specialtyjournal of Addictive Diseases." *18* 2, no. 23–37 (1999): 10.1300/J069v18n02_03.

Hughes, T. L., M. Howard, and D. Henry. "Comparison of Alcohol and Drug Use by Nurses and Other Occupational Groups." *Substance Use and Misuse* 37, no. 11 (2002): 1423–40.

Joranson, D., K. Ryan, A. Gilson, and J. Dahl. "Trends in Medical Use and Abuse of Opioid Analgesics." *Journal of American Medical Association* 283 (2000): 1710–14.

Kenna, G. A., and M. D. Wood. "Substance Use by Pharmacy and Nursing Practitioners and Students in a Northeastern State." *American Journal of Health-System Pharmacy* 61, no. 9 (2004): 921–30.

Lex, B. W. "Alcohol and Other Drug Abuse among Women." *Alcohol Research and Health* 18 (1994): 212–19.

Markel, H. *An Anatomy of Addiction: Sigmund Freud, William Halsted and the Miracle Drug, Cocaine.* New York: Pantheon Books, 2012.

Marnewick, J. C., and A. W. Van Zyl. "Substance Abuse among Oral Healthcare Workers." *South African Dental Journal* 69, no. 4 (2014): 148–52.

Martin, J. K., J. M. Kraft, and P. M. Roman. "Extent and Impact of Alcohol and Drug Use Problems in the Workplace: A Review of the Empirical Evidence." In *Drug Testing in the Workplace*, edited by S. Macdonald and P. M. Roman, 3–31. New York: Plenum Press, 1994.

Merlo, L. J., S. M. Cummings, and L. B. Cottler. "Recovering Substance-Impaired Pharmacists' Views Regarding Occupational Risks for Addiction." *Journal of the American Pharmacists Association* 22, no. 6 (2012): 605–12.

Morrison, J. *Dsm-5® Made Easy: The Clinician's Guide to Diagnosis.* New York: The Guilford Press, 2014.

Mullaney, T. "Survey: Nurses under Dangerous Stress." *McKnight's Long-Term Care News* 35, no. 8 (2014): 10.

Naegle, M. A. "Drug and Alcohol Abuse in Nursing." *Nursing Life* 8, no. 1 (1988): 42.54.

———. "Mental Health and Substance-Related Health Care." In *Addictions and Substance Abuse: Strategies for Advanced Nursing Practice*, edited by M. Naegle and C. E. D'Avanzo, 271–303. Saddle River, NJ: Prentice Hall Health, 2001.

———. *Substance Abuse and Addiction among Registered Nurses* 2ed. New York: Springer Publishing Company, 2006.

National Council of State Boards of Nursing (NCSBN). "Substance Use Disorder in Nursing, a Resource Manual and Guidelines for Alternative and Disciplinary Monitoring Programs." (2011): 280. https://www.ncsbn.org/SUDN_11.pdf.

National Institute on Drug Abuse (NIDA). *Drug Abuse and Addiction: The Basics.* 2016. http://www.drugabuse.gov/publications/media-guide/science-drug-abuse-addiction-basics.

Paget, J. "What Becomes of Medical Students." *St. Bartholomew's Hospital Report* 5 (1869): 238–42.

Quinlan, Diana Crna M. A. "Peer Assistance Reaches Its 25th Year." [In English]. *AANA Journal* 77, no. 4 (Aug 2009
2014-03-22 2009): 254–8.

Rehm, J., B. Taylor, and Room. R. "Global Burden of Disease from Alcohol, Illicit Drugs and Tobacco." *Drug and Alcohol Review* 25 (2006): 503–13.

Rojas, J. I., M. Brand, H. Jeon-Slaughter, and E. Koos. "Substance Abuse Patterns and Psychiatric Symptomology among Health Care Professionals and Non–Health Care Professionals Evaluated in an Outpatient Program for Impaired Professionals." *Addictive Disorders & Their Treatment* 13, no. 2 (2014): 45–53.

Room, R. "Stigma, Social Inequality and Alcohol and Drug Use." *Drug Alcohol Review* 24 (2005): 143–55.

Rose, J., M. Campbell, and G. Skipper. "Prognosis for Emergency Physician with Substance Abuse Recovery: 5-Year Outcome Study." *Western Journal of Emergency Medicine* 15, no. 1 (2014): 20–25.

Shaw, M. F., M. P. McGovern, D. H. Angres, and P. Rawal. "Physicians and Nurses with Substance Use Disorders." *Journal of Advanced Nursing* 47 (2004): 561–71.

Singer, M., and J. B. Page. *The Social Value of Drug Addicts: The Uses of the Useless.* Walnut Creek, CA: Left Coast Press, 2013.

Skipper, G. E., M. D. Campbell, and R. L. Dupont. "Anesthesiologists with Substance Use Disorders: A 5-Year Outcome Study from 16 State Physician Health Programsanesthesia Analgesi." *109*, no. 891–896 (2009).

Spicer, R. S., T. R. Miller, and G. S. Smith. "Worker Substance Use Workplace Problems and the Risk of Occupational Injury: A Matched Case-Control Study." *Quarterly Journal of Studies on Alcohol* 64 (2003): 570–78.

Stepter, N. R. "Drug Abuse among Nurses." *Nursing Management* 13, no. 12 (1982): 41–43.

Trinkoff, A. M., and C. L. Storr. "Substance Use among Nurses: Differences between Specialties." *American Journal of Public Health* 88 (1998a): 581–86.

———. "Work Schedule Characteristics and Substance Use in Nurses." *American Journal of Industrial Medicine* 34 (1998b): 266–71.

U.S. Department of Health and Human Services Health Resources and Services Administration. (HRSA). *Preliminary Findings: 2013 National Sample Survey of Registered Nurses.* 2013. http://bhpr.hrsa.gov/healthworkforce/reports/nursingworkforce/nursingworkforcefull-report.pdf.

White House. "Epidemic: Responding to America's Prescription Drug Abuse Crisis." Washington, DC: Office of the National Drug Control Policy, 2011.

White, W. L. "The Role of Recovering Physicians in 19th Century Addiction Medicine: An Organizational Case Study." *Journal of Addictive Diseases* 19, no. 2 (2000): 1–10.

Wilbert, M. I. "The Number and Kind of Drug Addicts." *Public Health Reports (1896-1970)* 30 (1915): 2289–94.

Wolfgang, A. P. "Job Stress in the Health Professions. A Study of Physicians, Nurses and Pharmacists." *Behavioral Medicine* 14, no. 1 (1988): 43–47.

Chapter Five

Nurses and Substance Use Disorders

Some studies suggest that the number of nurses who abuse drugs is comparable to that of the general public, while others have indicated that these percentages are significantly higher in the nursing population.[1] In the United States, professional training and education began for individuals to become professional nurses after the Civil War. The education and standard component of nurse curriculum followed the Florence Nightingale model.[2] This model embodied some of the most important traits in nursing—self-sacrifice, dedication, abstinence, and training—which would later be a symbol of the nurse profession.[3] Because of the self-sacrificing requirements of the profession and due to the stresses of the role, nurses may be vulnerable to self-destructive life patterns.[4] The image of the nurse as a healer of others' pain and the need for self-sacrifice in service to others have been identified as the trademarks of the nurse.[5] While nurturing and caring for an individual should support a nurse's empowerment, too often nursing has been practiced within bureaucratic organizations that promote disempowerment and promote codependency.[6] There is not a culture of safety in hospitals that would encourage nurses to show concern and speak up in support of one another.[7]

Since the early 1980s, both harmful practice and a substance abuse crisis surrounding nursing have been major issues[8] and have brought about a great deal of public attention.[9] Substance use disorders gained further public awareness when the American Nurses Association (ANA) addressed the issue defining that a nurse abusing substances is an impaired nurse whose professional judgment is affected by alcohol or drug misuse and who may jeopardize the delivery of high-quality safe care.[10]

Early studies suggested that substance use disorders are underreported in nurses and harder to estimate because of their ability to move from job to job and the lack of education, culture of mistreatment, or stigma in the workplace.[11] This causes nurses to conceal their substance use disorder and not seek treatment. Due to the stigma associated with the disease, determining the actual number of those who have substance use disorders continues to be difficult.[12] Therefore, the data that is being reported is data of nurses who have been disciplined for substance use and abuse. It does not reflect those receiving general treatment and treatment through alternatives to discipline programs. Also, when an individual is labeled a substance abuser, this individual is more likely to receive a punitive response rather than a therapeutic response to their disease.[13] Nurses receive greater punitive responses from regulatory boards than their physician counterparts. The rate at which nurses are disciplined prior to treatment is higher than physicians, and after treatment, nurses are disciplined disproportionately at 35% higher than physicians.[14] The denial and stigma that perpetuates substance use disorders, along with the high expectation and trust afforded the nursing professions, may be the reason nurses with substance use disorders choose to remain silent and not seek treatment, or treatment at the same rate as the general public.[15]

SUBSTANCE ABUSE, AN OCCUPATIONAL HAZARD FOR NURSES

Throughout the 20th century and into the 21st century, increased knowledge and understanding of the causes and processes of sickness and disease, the development and expansion of medical and health services, and the changing patterns of modern life have not only extended the scope of nurses' work but have also made nursing a more highly complex and stressful occupation.[16] Nurses report more on the job stress than other health care professionals.[17]

Stressful work, staff shortages, and increased acuteness and patient ratios, in parallel with easy access to drugs and self-medicating, have led some nurses into misusing drugs. Additionally, occupational schedules that combine longer shifts and shift rotations are the schedules most associated with substance abuse.[18] These adverse work schedules combined with domestic requirements at home increase nurse fatigue, stress, and sleep deprivation; such schedules, most likely to occur in hospital settings, lead to fatigue and other negative physiological and psychological outcomes for the nurse.[19]

Setting areas where the work-related stress is greater, such as those surrounding neurosurgical nursing that exposes nurses to life and death situations and can be short of essential resources and staff, affect work performance and are considered major stress factors.[20] For example, an early study of 4,438 registered nurses revealed that nurses working in critical care and the emergency room reported being more likely to use drugs, marijuana, and cocaine than nurses in other less stressful settings.[21] The very character, environment, and stress of the nursing profession may encourage substance use as a way of coping. Substance use disorders affect the families and friends of nurses dealing with use and abuse, as well as their coworkers and patients.[22]

Signs and Symptoms of Substance Use Disorders

Although there are symptoms and signs of substance abuse by nurses in the workplace, many times these are ignored or unrecognized by other healthcare professionals.[23] Signs and symptoms of substance use disorders can range from very subtle to extremely obvious.[24] Nurses with substance use disorders often use before and during their shifts.[25] Signs of use may include increased absenteeism; leaving the unit for excessive amounts of time; spending more time around medication carts and rooms; and impairment in judgment and work performance.[26] While the signs are there, research has suggested that substance abuse impairment may be difficult to identify. A quasi-experimental study of 120 nursing students, conducted by Boulton and Nosek,[27] revealed that less than half the students indicated they could recognize impairment in a colleague. Further, they indicated they had not received adequate education regarding substance abuse. This lack of awareness and education makes nurses reluctant to confront a colleague suffering from a substance use disorder. This is concerning, as colleagues appear to have little knowledge about something that is likely to affect them directly or indirectly at some time in their career.[28]

Not just students or nursing staff, but other studies found that Directors of Nursing and nurse managers were not able to distinguish warning signs of substance abuse among other nursing professionals.[29] This is troubling as it is particularly important that nurse managers gain the basic understanding of the signs and symptoms of substance use disorders, as they play a vital role in managing a nurse whose practice may be affected due to substance abuse.[30] Nurse managers need to be able to identify and address nurses who are impaired in a systematic manner to limit the negative impact on patients and threat to the safety of coworkers.[31]

Justification for Drug Use

Nurses with substance use disorders frequently did not view themselves objectively and believed they were justified in using substances.[32] Affected nurses may rationalize their behavior and rely on a set of implicit biases to justify their substance use. These biases are labeled as the "justification of mechanisms of addiction."[33] For example, in one bias, the person has the tendency to regard behavior patterns and life choices as involuntary. This individual sees himself or herself as a victim powerless to resist the recurring onslaught of compelling urges.[34] One of the major trademarks of addiction or a substance use disorder is an individual's willingness to continue with behaviors that are self-destructive or self-defeating despite the consequences to the individual's quality of life.[35] This specifically relates to nurses who start diverting medications for personal reasons. The job stress and pain they experience can be the gateway into addiction.[36] They may succumb to the urges and rationalize and minimize the seriousness of diverting by claiming the medication was going to be wasted anyhow.[37] Research suggests they may also justify their behavior by believing they are not harming anyone. Yet, substance use disorder is a disease that is destructive, progressive, and persistent despite all consequences.[38] It threatens professional standards and the delivery of quality care and, if rationalization continues and substance use and abuse are left unchecked, it can lead to grave consequences for healthcare consumers.[39]

Early Indicators and Risk Factor in Nurses

Nurses, similar to other healthcare workers are at greater risk for using or abusing substances if they have a family history of alcoholism, drug use and abuse, emotional abuse or harm, which can result in overwork, overachievement or low self-esteem.[40] Substance abusing nurses often hold demanding responsible positions, are considered high performers, rank near the top of their classes, have advanced degrees, have great esteem from their colleagues, and come from families that have at least one parent who is a substance abuser.[41] In a study of 100 nurses with substance use disorders and 100 nurses without substance use disorders, differences in the early risk indicators were significant for both sensation-seeking behaviors and a family history of drug and alcohol use.[42] Nurses would obtain greater insight if they could identify their personal risk factors early in their careers (e.g., family history risk factors) for "substance-related disorders" and could use this insight to control their inclination for substance use and abuse.[43]

Nurses and nursing students reported the highest percentages of family members with drug problems; this was followed by pharmacists, physicians, and dentists.[44] This along with physical and emotional abuse, low self-esteem, psychological stress, weak religious affiliations, high abuse among peers, sensation-seeking behaviors, and early age use have also been identified as predictors of substance use disorders.[45]

Nurses' familiarity and knowledge about substances may also lead them to "pharmacological optimism,"[46] a belief and attitude that substance use is an acceptable way of changing one's emotional state.[47] Additionally, familiarity and knowledge about substances may similarly lead them to a sense of "pharmaceutical invincibility," which is the feeling they are immune to the addictive effects of drugs.[48] These beliefs along with physical access to drugs can influence nurses to make the choice to self-medicate.

NOTES

1. D. Dunn, "Substance Abuse among Nurses – Intercession and Intervention," Association of Operating Room Nurses Journal 82, no. 2 (2005); Susanne Astrab Fogger and Teena McGuinness, "Alabama's Nurse Monitoring Programs: The Nurse's Experience of Being Monitored," Journal of Addictions Nursing 20, no. 3 (2009); T. B. Monroe and H. Kenaga, "Don't Ask Don't Tell: Substance Abuse and Addiction among Nurses," Journal of Clinical Nursing 20 (2010); National Council of State Boards of Nursing (NCSBN), "Substance Use Disorder in Nursing, a Resource Manual and Guidelines for Alternative and Disciplinary Monitoring Programs," (2011), https://www.ncsbn.org/SUDN_11.pdf; A. Reber-Frantz, "A Policy Analysis of Nursing Students with Criminal Backgrounds in the State of California: Need for a Standardized Screening Process to Improve Efficiency and Enhance Public Safety " (Doctoral dissertation, Western University of Health Sciences, 2014).
2. B. Heise, "The Historical Context of Addiction in the Nursing Profession: 1850–1982," Journal of Addictions Nurse 14, no. 3 (2003).
3. E. F. Pollard, Florence Nightingale: The Wounded Soldier's Friend; Fully Illustrated, (London: S. W. Partridge and Co. Ltd., 1911), http://hdl.handle.net/2027/uc2.ark:/13960/t3qv3tp56; J. G. Widerquist, "The Spirituality of Florence Nightingale," PDF only, Nursing Research 41, no. 1 (1992).
4. J. L. Bowler, M. C. Bowler, and L. R. James, "The Cognitive Underpinnings of Addiction," Substance Use & Misuse 46 (2011); A. M. Trinkoff et al., "Workplace Access, Negative Prescription, Job Strain, and Substance Use in Registered Nurses," Nursing Research 49, no. 2 (2000).
5. E. J. Pask, "Self-Sacrifice, Self-Transcendence and Nurses' Professional Self," Nursing Philosophy: An International Journal for Healthcare Professionals, no. 6 (2005); Trinkoff et al., "Workplace Access, Negative Prescription, Job Strain, and Substance Use in Registered Nurses."
6. R. A. Caffrey and P. A. Caffrey, "Nursing: Caring or Codependent?," Nursing Forum 29, no. 1 (1994).
7. D. Maxfield et al., "Silence Kills–the Seven Crucial Conversations for Healthcare," Vital Smarts (2005).
8. L. L. Smith, "The Role of the Nurse Manager," in National Council for State Boards of Nursing, Chemical Dependency Handbook for Nurse Managers: A Guide for Managing Chemically Dependent Employees, ed. L. L. Smith (Chicago, IL: National Council Publisher, 2001).
9. L. Blazer and P. Mansfield, "A Comparison of Substance Use Rates among Female Nurses, Clerical Workers and Blue-Collar Workers," Journal of Advanced Nursing 21, no. 2 (1995); A. M. Trinkoff, W. W. Eaton, and J. C. Anthony, "The Prevalence of Substance Abuse among Registered Nurses," Nursing Research 40, no. 3 (1991).
10. American Nurses' Association, Addictions and Psychological Dysfunctions in Nursing: The Profession's Response to the Problem (Kansas, MO: American Nurses' Association, 1984).
11. N. Darbro, "Alternative Diversion Programs for Nurses with Impaired Practice: Completers and Non-Completers," Journal of Addictions Nursing 16, no. 4 (2005); S. Garb, "Narcotic Addiction in Nurses and Doctors," Nursing Outlook 13, no. 11 (1965).
12. Reber-Frantz, "A Policy Analysis of Nursing Students with Criminal Backgrounds in the State of California: Need for a Standardized Screening Process to Improve Efficiency and Enhance Public Safety."
13. J. F. Kelly, S. Dow, and C. Westerhoff, "Does It Matter How We Refer to Individuals with Substance-Related Conditions? A Randomized Study of Two Commonly Used Terms," International Journal of Drug Policy 21, no. 3 (2009).

14. M. F. Shaw et al., "Physicians and Nurses with Substance Use Disorders," Journal of Advanced Nursing 47 (2004).

15. T. B. Monroe et al., "The Prevalence of Employed Nurses Identified or Enrolled in Substance Use Monitoring Programs," Nurse Research 62, no. 1 (2013); National Council of State Boards of Nursing (NCSBN), "Substance Use Disorder in Nursing, a Resource Manual and Guidelines for Alternative and Disciplinary Monitoring Programs"; S. Shaffer, "Attitudes and Perceptions Held by Impaired Nurses: There Is Urgent Need Both for Concern and Action in Assisting Nurses to Recover from Addiction," Nursing Management (Springhouse) 19, no. 4 (1988).

16. Shaw et al., "Physicians and Nurses with Substance Use Disorders."; J. Snape and S. J. Cavanagh, "Occupational Stress in Neurosurgical Nursing," Intensive and Critical Care Nursing 9, no. 3 (1993); A. P. Wolfgang, "Job Stress in the Health Professions. A Study of Physicians, Nurses and Pharmacists," Behavioral Medicine 14, no. 1 (1988).

17. M. A. Naegle, "Drug and Alcohol Abuse in Nursing," Nursing Life 8, no. 1 (1988); "Mental Health and Substance-Related Health Care," in Addictions and Substance Abuse: Strategies for Advanced Nursing Practice, ed. M. Naegle and C. E. D'Avanzo (Saddle River, NJ: Prentice Hall Health, 2001); A. M. Trinkoff and C. L. Storr, "Work Schedule Characteristics and Substance Use in Nurses," American Journal of Industrial Medicine 34 (1998b).

18. Heise, "The Historical Context of Addiction in the Nursing Profession: 1850–1982."; National Council of State Boards of Nursing (NCSBN), "Substance Use Disorder in Nursing, a Resource Manual and Guidelines for Alternative and Disciplinary Monitoring Programs."

19. J. Geiger-Brown and A. M. Trinkoff, "Is It Time to Pull the Plug on 12-Hour Shifts for Nurses?," Journal of Nursing Administration 40 (2010); K. Han, A. M. Trinkoff, and J. Geiger-Brown, "Factors Associated with Work-Related Fatigue and Recovery in Hospital Nurses Working 12-Hour Shifts," Workplace Health & Safety 62 (2014).

20. Snape and Cavanagh, "Occupational Stress in Neurosurgical Nursing."

21. A. M. Trinkoff and C. L. Storr, "Substance Use among Nurses: Differences between Specialties," American Journal of Public Health 88 (1998a).

22. C. J. Cherpitel, "Alcohol and Injuries: A Review of International Emergency Room Studies since 1995," Drug and Alcohol Review 26 (2007); R. B. Coambs and M. P. McAndrews, "The Effects of Psychoactive Substances on Workplace Performance," in Drug Testing in the Workplace, ed. S. Macdonald and P. M. Roman, Research Advances in Alcohol and Drug Problems (Boston, MA: Springer, 1994); S. Cohen, "Drugs in the Workplace," Journal of Clinical Psychiatry 45 (1984); M. R. Frone, "Alcohol, Drugs, and Workplace Safety Outcomes: A View from a General Model of Employee Substance Use and Productivity," in The Psychology of Workplace Safety ed. J. Barling and M. R. Frone (Washington, DC: American Psychological Association, 2004); "Employee Alcohol and Illicit Drug Use: Scope, Causes and Organizational Consequences," in Handbook of Organizational Behavior, ed. C. L. Cooper and J. Barling (Thousand Oaks, CA: Sage Publications, 2009); S. W. Gust et al., eds., Drugs in the Workplace: Research and Evaluation Data Nida Research Monograph No. 100 (Rockville, MD: U.S. Department of Health & Human Services, 1990); J. K. Martin, J. M. Kraft, and P. M. Roman, "Extent and Impact of Alcohol and Drug Use Problems in the Workplace: A Review of the Empirical Evidence," in Drug Testing in the Workplace, ed. S. Macdonald and P. M. Roman (New York: Plenum Press, 1994); J. Rehm, B. Taylor, and Room. R., "Global Burden of Disease from Alcohol, Illicit Drugs and Tobacco," Drug and Alcohol Review 25 (2006); R. S. Spicer, T. R. Miller, and G. S. Smith, "Worker Substance Use Workplace Problems and the Risk of Occupational Injury: A Matched Case-Control Study," Quarterly Journal of Studies on Alcohol 64 (2003).

23. M. A. Boulton and L. J. Nosek, "How Do Nursing Students Perceive Substance Abusing Nurses?," Archives of psychiatric nursing 28, no. 1 (2014); G. A. McKenna, "Diagnosis and Treatment of Substance Use Disorder in Professionals," Hawaii Dental Journal 36, no. 4 (2005).

24. K. H. Berge, M. D. Seppala, and A. M. Schipper, "Chemical Dependency and the Physician," Mayo Clinic Proceedings 84, no. 7 (2009).

25. S. Ponech, "Signs," Nursing Management 31, no. 5 (2000).

26. Drug Enforcement Administration (DEA), Drug Addiction in Healthcare Professionals, (2008), http://www.deadiversion.usdoj.gov; National Council of State Boards of Nursing (NCSBN), "Substance Use Disorder in Nursing, a Resource Manual and Guidelines for Alternative and Disciplinary Monitoring Programs"; J. J. Talbert, "Substance Abuse among Nurses," Clinical Journal of Oncology Nursing 13, no. 1 (2009).

27. Boulton and Nosek, "How Do Nursing Students Perceive Substance Abusing Nurses?"

28. D. Quinlan, "Impaired Nursing Practice: A National Perspective on Peer Assistance in the U.S.," Journal of Addictions Nursing 14, no. 149–155 (2003).

29. McKenna, "Diagnosis and Treatment of Substance Use Disorder in Professionals."

30. National Council of State Boards of Nursing (NCSBN), "Substance Use Disorder in Nursing, a Resource Manual and Guidelines for Alternative and Disciplinary Monitoring Programs."

31. L. T. Kohn, J. M. Corrigan, and M. S. Donaldson, eds., To Err Is Human: Building a Safer Health System (Washington, DC: National Academy Press, 2000).

32. Bowler, Bowler, and James, "The Cognitive Underpinnings of Addiction."

33. Ibid., 1061–62.

34. J. Balmford and R. Borland, "What Does It Mean to Want to Quit?," Drug and Alcohol Review 2008, no. 27 (2008); J. Mendelson and N. Mello, The Addictive Personality (New York: Chelsea House, 1986); J. A. Schaler, Addiction Is a Choice (Chicago, IL: Open Court Publishing, 2000).

35. Bowler, Bowler, and James, "The Cognitive Underpinnings of Addiction."

36. D. Busch, A. B. McBride, and L. M. Benaventura, "Chemical Dependency in Women: The Link to Ob/Gyn Problems," Journal of Psychosocial Nursing and Mental Health Services 24, no. 4 (1986); T. A. Hickman, The Secret Leprosy of Modern Days: Narcotic Addiction and Cultural Crisis in the United States, 1870–1920 (Amherst, MA: University of Massachusetts Press, 2007); B. W. Lex, "Alcohol and Other Drug Abuse among Women," Alcohol Research and Health 18 (1994); N. R. Stepter, "Drug Abuse among Nurses," Nursing Management 13, no. 12 (1982); Trinkoff et al., "Workplace Access, Negative Prescription, Job Strain, and Substance Use in Registered Nurses."

37. P. Maher-Brisen, "Addiction: An Occupational Hazard in Nursing," The American Journal of Nursing 107, no. 8 (2007).

38. G. F. Koob and M. Le Moal, "Addiction and the Brain Antireward System," Annual Review of Psychology 59 (2008).

39. L. Bissell and P. W. Haberman, Alcoholism in the Professions (New York: Oxford University Press, 1984); E. Sullivan, L. Bissell, and E. Williams, "Chemical Dependency in Nursing: The Deadly Diversion," The American Journal of Nursing 88 (1988).

40. G. Monahan, "Drug Use/Misuse among Health Professionals," Substance Use & Misuse 38 (2003).

41. J. O. S. I. E. O'Quinn-Larson and M. R. Pickard, "The Impaired Nursing Student," Nurse Educator 14, no. 2 (1989).

42. M. M. West, "Early Risk Indicators of Substance Abuse among Nurses," Journal of Nursing Scholarship 34, no. 2 (2002).

43. Ibid., 187.

44. Bissell and Haberman, Alcoholism in the Professions; L. Bugle, "A Study of Drug and Alcohol Use among Missouri Rns," Journal of Psychosocial Nursing and Mental Health Services 34 (1996); G. A. Kenna and M. D. Wood, "Family History of Alcoholism and Alcohol Use in College Healthcare Students" (paper presented at the 72nd Annual Eastern Psychological Association Convention, Washington DC, March 23–25, 2000 2000); "Family History of Alcohol and Drug Use in Healthcare Professionals," Journal of Substance Use 10 (2005); K. Kriegler, J. Baldwin, and D. Scott, "Journal of American College Health," 42, no. 259–265 (1994A survey of alcohol and other drug use behaviors and risk factors health profession students); S. L. Mynatt, "A Model of Contributing Risk Factors to Chemical Dependency in Nurses," Journal of Psychosocial Nursing and Mental Health Services 34, no. 7 (1996); E. Sullivan, "Comparison of Chemically Dependent and Nondependent Nurses on Familial, Personal and Professional Characteristics," Journal on Studies of Alcohol 48 (1987); N. Valentine,

"Stress, Alcohol and Psychoactive Drug Use among Nurses in Massachusetts " (Unpublished doctoral dissertation, Brandeis University, Boston, 1991).

45. B. H. Bry, "Predicting Drug Abuse: Review and Reformulation," International Journal of Addiction 18 (1983); L. J. Francis and K. Mullen, "Religiosity and Attitudes Towards Drug Use among 13–15 Year Olds in England," Addiction 88 (1993); E. R. Galaif and M. D. Newcomb, "Predictors of Polydrug Use among Four Ethnic Groups: A 12-Year Longitudinal Study," Addictive Behaviors 24 (1999); P. H. Hughes, "Prevention of Prescription Drug Abuse: An Educational Approach," in Sixth Southeastern Conference on Prescription Drug Abuse (Tampa, FL 1990); Kenna and Wood, "Family History of Alcohol and Drug Use in Healthcare Professionals."; S. L. Mynatt, "Increasing Resiliency to Substance Abuse in Recovering Women with Comorbid Depression," Journal of Psychosocial Nursing and Mental Health Services 3, no. 1 (1998); A. M. Trinkoff and C. L. Storr, "Relationship of Specialty and Access to Substance Use among Registered Nurses: An Exploratory Analysis," Drug and Alcohol Dependence 36 (1994); West, "Early Risk Indicators of Substance Abuse among Nurses."

46. Trinkoff et al., "Workplace Access, Negative Prescription, Job Strain, and Substance Use in Registered Nurses," 83.

47. J. M. Brewster, Drug Use among Canadian Professionals (Ottawa, Canada: Minister of National Health and Welfare, 1994); M. Buxton, "Three-Step Recovery Model Aids Impaired Nurses," Hospital Employee Health 1 (1982); Trinkoff et al., "Workplace Access, Negative Prescription, Job Strain, and Substance Use in Registered Nurses."

48. G. A. Kenna and D. C. Lewis, "Risk Factors for Alcohol and Other Drug Use by Healthcare Professionals," Substance Abuse Treatment, Prevention, and Policy 3, no. 1 (2008): 1.

BIBLIOGRAPHY

American Nurses' Association. *Addictions and Psychological Dysfunctions in Nursing: The Profession's Response to the Problem.* Kansas, MO: American Nurses' Association, 1984.

Balmford, J., and R. Borland. "What Does It Mean to Want to Quit?" *Drug and Alcohol Review* 2008, no. 27 (2008): 21–27.

Berge, K. H., M. D. Seppala, and A. M. Schipper. "Chemical Dependency and the Physician." *Mayo Clinic Proceedings* 84, no. 7 (2009): 625–31.

Bissell, L., and P. W. Haberman. *Alcoholism in the Professions.* New York: Oxford University Press, 1984.

Blazer, L., and P. Mansfield. "A Comparison of Substance Use Rates among Female Nurses, Clerical Workers and Blue-Collar Workers." *Journal of Advanced Nursing* 21, no. 2 (1995): 305–13.

Boulton, M. A., and L. J. Nosek. "How Do Nursing Students Perceive Substance Abusing Nurses?" *Archives of psychiatric nursing* 28, no. 1 (2014): 29–34.

Bowler, J. L., M. C. Bowler, and L. R. James. "The Cognitive Underpinnings of Addiction." *Substance Use & Misuse* 46 (2011): 1060–70.

Brewster, J. M. *Drug Use among Canadian Professionals.* Ottawa, Canada: Minister of National Health and Welfare, 1994.

Bry, B. H. "Predicting Drug Abuse: Review and Reformulation." *International Journal of Addiction* 18 (1983): 223–33.

Bugle, L. "A Study of Drug and Alcohol Use among Missouri Rns." *Journal of Psychosocial Nursing and Mental Health Services* 34 (1996): 41–45.

Busch, D., A. B. McBride, and L. M. Benaventura. "Chemical Dependency in Women: The Link to Ob/Gyn Problems." *Journal of Psychosocial Nursing and Mental Health Services* 24, no. 4 (1986): 26–30.

Buxton, M. "Three-Step Recovery Model Aids Impaired Nurses." *Hospital Employee Health* 1 (1982): 24–27.

Caffrey, R. A., and P. A. Caffrey. "Nursing: Caring or Codependent?" *Nursing Forum* 29, no. 1 (1994): 12–16.

Cherpitel, C. J. "Alcohol and Injuries: A Review of International Emergency Room Studies since 1995." *Drug and Alcohol Review* 26 (2007): 201–14.

Coambs, R. B., and M. P. McAndrews. "The Effects of Psychoactive Substances on Workplace Performance." In *Drug Testing in the Workplace*, edited by S. Macdonald and P. M. Roman. Research Advances in Alcohol and Drug Problems, 77-102. Boston, MA: Springer, 1994.

Cohen, S. "Drugs in the Workplace." *Journal of Clinical Psychiatry* 45 (1984): 4–8.

Darbro, N. "Alternative Diversion Programs for Nurses with Impaired Practice: Completers and Non-Completers." *Journal of Addictions Nursing* 16, no. 4 (2005): 169–86.

Drug Enforcement Administration (DEA). *Drug Addiction in Healthcare Professionals*. 2008. http://www.deadiversion.usdoj.gov.

Dunn, D. "Substance Abuse among Nurses—Intercession and Intervention." *Association of Operating Room Nurses Journal* 82, no. 2 (2005): 87–88.

Fogger, Susanne Astrab, and Teena McGuinness. "Alabama's Nurse Monitoring Programs: The Nurse's Experience of Being Monitored." *Journal of Addictions Nursing* 20, no. 3 (2009/01/01 2009): 142–49.

Francis, L. J., and K. Mullen. "Religiosity and Attitudes Towards Drug Use among 13–15 Year Olds in England." *Addiction* 88 (1993): 665–72.

Frone, M. R. "Alcohol, Drugs, and Workplace Safety Outcomes: A View from a General Model of Employee Substance Use and Productivity." In *The Psychology of Workplace Safety* edited by J. Barling and M. R. Frone, 127–56. Washington, DC: American Psychological Association, 2004.

———. "Employee Alcohol and Illicit Drug Use: Scope, Causes and Organizational Consequences." In *Handbook of Organizational Behavior*, edited by C. L. Cooper and J. Barling. Thousand Oaks, CA: Sage Publications, 2009.

Galaif, E. R., and M. D. Newcomb. "Predictors of Polydrug Use among Four Ethnic Groups: A 12-Year Longitudinal Study." *Addictive Behaviors* 24 (1999): 607–31.

Garb, S. "Narcotic Addiction in Nurses and Doctors." *Nursing Outlook* 13, no. 11 (1965): 30–34.

Geiger-Brown, J., and A. M. Trinkoff. "Is It Time to Pull the Plug on 12-Hour Shifts for Nurses?" *Journal of Nursing Administration* 40 (2010): 357–59.

Gust, S. W., J. M. Walsh, L. B. Thomas, and D. J. Crouch, eds. *Drugs in the Workplace: Research and Evaluation Data* Nida Research Monograph No. 100. Rockville, MD: U.S. Department of Health & Human Services, 1990.

Han, K., A. M. Trinkoff, and J. Geiger-Brown. "Factors Associated with Work-Related Fatigue and Recovery in Hospital Nurses Working 12-Hour Shifts." *Workplace Health & Safety* 62 (2014): 409–14.

Heise, B. "The Historical Context of Addiction in the Nursing Profession: 1850-1982." *Journal of Addictions Nurse* 14, no. 3 (2003): 117–24.

Hickman, T. A. *The Secret Leprosy of Modern Days: Narcotic Addiction and Cultural Crisis in the United States, 1870–1920*. Amherst, MA: University of Massachusetts Press, 2007.

Hughes, P. H. "Prevention of Prescription Drug Abuse: An Educational Approach." In *Sixth Southeastern Conference on Prescription Drug Abuse*. Tampa, FL, 1990.

Kelly, J. F., S. Dow, and C. Westerhoff. "Does It Matter How We Refer to Individuals with Substance-Related Conditions? A Randomized Study of Two Commonly Used Terms." *International Journal of Drug Policy* 21, no. 3 (2009): 202–07.

Kenna, G. A., and D. C. Lewis. "Risk Factors for Alcohol and Other Drug Use by Healthcare Professionals." *Substance Abuse Treatment, Prevention, and Policy* 3, no. 1 (2008): 3.

Kenna, G. A., and M. D. Wood. "Family History of Alcohol and Drug Use in Healthcare Professionals." *Journal of Substance Use* 10 (2005): 225–38.

———. "Family History of Alcoholism and Alcohol Use in College Healthcare Students." Paper presented at the 72nd Annual Eastern Psychological Association Convention, Washington DC, March 23–25, 2000 2000.

Kohn, L. T., J. M. Corrigan, and M. S. Donaldson, eds. *To Err Is Human: Building a Safer Health System*. Washington, DC: National Academy Press, 2000.

Koob, G. F., and M. Le Moal. "Addiction and the Brain Antireward System." *Annual Review of Psychology* 59 (2008): 29–53.

Kriegler, K., J. Baldwin, and D. Scott. "Journal of American College Health." *42*, no. 259–265 (1994A survey of alcohol and other drug use behaviors and risk factors health profession students).

Lex, B. W. "Alcohol and Other Drug Abuse among Women." *Alcohol Research and Health* 18 (1994): 212–19.

Maher-Brisen, P. "Addiction: An Occupational Hazard in Nursing." *The American Journal of Nursing* 107, no. 8 (2007): 78–79.

Martin, J. K., J. M. Kraft, and P. M. Roman. "Extent and Impact of Alcohol and Drug Use Problems in the Workplace: A Review of the Empirical Evidence." In *Drug Testing in the Workplace*, edited by S. Macdonald and P. M. Roman, 3–31. New York: Plenum Press, 1994.

Maxfield, D., J. Grenny, R. McMillan, K. Patterson, and A. Switzler. "Silence Kills–the Seven Crucial Conversations for Healthcare." *Vital Smarts* (2005): E5.

McKenna, G. A. "Diagnosis and Treatment of Substance Use Disorder in Professionals." *Hawaii Dental Journal* 36, no. 4 (2005): 13–15.

Mendelson, J., and N. Mello. *The Addictive Personality.* New York: Chelsea House, 1986.

Monahan, G. "Drug Use/Misuse among Health Professionals." *Substance Use & Misuse* 38 (2003): 1877–81.

Monroe, T. B., and H. Kenaga. "Don't Ask Don't Tell: Substance Abuse and Addiction among Nurses." *Journal of Clinical Nursing* 20 (2010): 504–09.

Monroe, T. B., H. Kenaga, M. S. Dietrich, M. A. Carter, and R. L Cowan. "The Prevalence of Employed Nurses Identified or Enrolled in Substance Use Monitoring Programs." *Nurse Research* 62, no. 1 (2013): 10–15.

Mynatt, S. L. "Increasing Resiliency to Substance Abuse in Recovering Women with Comorbid Depression." *Journal of Psychosocial Nursing and Mental Health Services* 3, no. 1 (1998): 28–36.

———. "A Model of Contributing Risk Factors to Chemical Dependency in Nurses." *Journal of Psychosocial Nursing and Mental Health Services* 34, no. 7 (1996): 13–22.

Naegle, M. A. "Drug and Alcohol Abuse in Nursing." *Nursing Life* 8, no. 1 (1988): 42.54.

———. "Mental Health and Substance-Related Health Care." In *Addictions and Substance Abuse: Strategies for Advanced Nursing Practice*, edited by M. Naegle and C. E. D'Avanzo, 271–303. Saddle River, NJ: Prentice Hall Health, 2001.

National Council of State Boards of Nursing (NCSBN). "Substance Use Disorder in Nursing, a Resource Manual and Guidelines for Alternative and Disciplinary Monitoring Programs." (2011): 280. https://www.ncsbn.org/SUDN_11.pdf.

O'Quinn-Larson, J. O. S. I. E., and M. R. Pickard. "The Impaired Nursing Student." *Nurse Educator* 14, no. 2 (1989): 36–39.

Pask, E. J. "Self-Sacrifice, Self-Transcendence and Nurses' Professional Self." Nursing Philosophy: An International Journal for Healthcare Professionals, no. 6 (2005).

Pollard, E. F. *Florence Nightingale: The Wounded Soldier's Friend; Fully Illustrated.* London: S. W. Partridge and Co. Ltd., 1911. http://hdl.handle.net/2027/uc2.ark:/13960/t3qv3tp56.

Ponech, S. "Signs." *Nursing Management* 31, no. 5 (2000): 32–38.

Quinlan, D. "Impaired Nursing Practice: A National Perspective on Peer Assistance in the U.S." *Journal of Addictions Nursing* 14, no. 149–155 (2003).

Reber-Frantz, A. "A Policy Analysis of Nursing Students with Criminal Backgrounds in the State of California: Need for a Standardized Screening Process to Improve Efficiency and Enhance Public Safety " Doctoral dissertation, Western University of Health Sciences, 2014.

Rehm, J., B. Taylor, and Room. R. "Global Burden of Disease from Alcohol, Illicit Drugs and Tobacco." *Drug and Alcohol Review* 25 (2006): 503–13.

Schaler, J. A. *Addiction Is a Choice.* Chicago, IL: Open Court Publishing, 2000.

Shaffer, S. "Attitudes and Perceptions Held by Impaired Nurses: There Is Urgent Need Both for Concern and Action in Assisting Nurses to Recover from Addiction." *Nursing Management (Springhouse)* 19, no. 4 (1988): 46–51.

Shaw, M. F., M. P. McGovern, D. H. Angres, and P. Rawal. "Physicians and Nurses with Substance Use Disorders." *Journal of Advanced Nursing* 47 (2004): 561–71.

Smith, L. L. "The Role of the Nurse Manager." In *National Council for State Boards of Nursing, Chemical Dependency Handbook for Nurse Managers: A Guide for Managing Chemically Dependent Employees*, edited by L. L. Smith, 21–28. Chicago, IL: National Council Publisher, 2001.

Snape, J., and S. J. Cavanagh. "Occupational Stress in Neurosurgical Nursing." *Intensive and Critical Care Nursing* 9, no. 3 (1993): 162–70.

Spicer, R. S., T. R. Miller, and G. S. Smith. "Worker Substance Use Workplace Problems and the Risk of Occupational Injury: A Matched Case-Control Study." *Quarterly Journal of Studies on Alcohol* 64 (2003): 570–78.

Stepter, N. R. "Drug Abuse among Nurses." *Nursing Management* 13, no. 12 (1982): 41–43.

Sullivan, E. "Comparison of Chemically Dependent and Nondependent Nurses on Familial, Personal and Professional Characteristics." *Journal on Studies of Alcohol* 48 (1987): 563–68.

Sullivan, E., L. Bissell, and E. Williams. "Chemical Dependency in Nursing: The Deadly Diversion." *The American Journal of Nursing* 88 (1988): 1597.

Talbert, J. J. "Substance Abuse among Nurses." *Clinical Journal of Oncology Nursing* 13, no. 1 (2009): 17–19.

Trinkoff, A. M., W. W. Eaton, and J. C. Anthony. "The Prevalence of Substance Abuse among Registered Nurses." *Nursing Research* 40, no. 3 (1991): 172–74.

Trinkoff, A. M., Q. Shou, C. L. Storr, and K. L. Soeken. "Workplace Access, Negative Prescription, Job Strain, and Substance Use in Registered Nurses." *Nursing Research* 49, no. 2 (2000): 83–90.

Trinkoff, A. M., and C. L. Storr. "Relationship of Specialty and Access to Substance Use among Registered Nurses: An Exploratory Analysis." *Drug and Alcohol Dependence* 36 (1994): 215–19.

———. "Substance Use among Nurses: Differences between Specialties." *American Journal of Public Health* 88 (1998a): 581–86.

———. "Work Schedule Characteristics and Substance Use in Nurses." *American Journal of Industrial Medicine* 34 (1998b): 266–71.

Valentine, N. "Stress, Alcohol and Psychoactive Drug Use among Nurses in Massachusetts " Unpublished doctoral dissertation, Brandeis University, Boston, 1991.

West, M. M. "Early Risk Indicators of Substance Abuse among Nurses." *Journal of Nursing Scholarship* 34, no. 2 (2002): 187–93.

Widerquist, J. G. "The Spirituality of Florence Nightingale." PDF only, *Nursing Research* 41, no. 1 (1992): 49–55.

Wolfgang, A. P. "Job Stress in the Health Professions. A Study of Physicians, Nurses and Pharmacists." *Behavioral Medicine* 14, no. 1 (1988): 43–47.

Chapter Six

Nursing Students and Nursing Schools

Many nurses started having substance abuse problems while in nursing school.[1] Indicators of substance use risks have been acknowledged in studies of nursing students suggesting that some of these individuals were suffering from substance use disorders before entering nursing school.[2] Prescription drug abuse has been suggested to be the most problematic for nursing students.[3] National Institute on Drug Abuse (NIDA)[4] data show that individuals ranging between 18 and 25 have the highest rates of prescription drug abuse, which coincides with the age of most first-time college students. Student nurses' access to the prescriptions, stressful working conditions, and their experiences and education regarding prescription drugs have been found to be contributing factors.[5] Although the American Association of Colleges of Nurses (AACN) promotes treatment and rehabilitation, many nursing schools traditionally follow a policy of "zero-tolerance" and dismiss students with substance use disorders from nursing training programs.[6]

Nursing schools are the gateway into the nursing profession. The schools are well positioned to be the first area of prevention and defense against the occupational hazards that substance use disorders in nursing have become. Yet, most nursing school curricula include little content on substance use disorders.[7] An early systematic review of substance abuse education in nursing schools revealed that nursing students received substantially less substance abuse training in their academic programs than other health-care professionals.[8] More recent research has suggested there continues to be a gap in the education of nursing students regarding the risks of substance use disorders within the nursing profession.[9] A newly licensed nurse's effectiveness on dealing with a coworker suspected of substance misuse and abuse is limited by the lack of information about substance use disorders in nursing school.[10] However, when an educational seminar regarding substance abuse was provided, a study of nursing students using a pretest-posttest survey evaluation revealed that this type of seminar made an impact on the students' increased knowledge in identifying and intervening with a colleague with substance use disorders.[11] Requiring information related to substance use and abuse as part of the curriculum in nursing schools may limit the impact of substance use disorders in the nursing profession.[12] More effective policies and education are needed in nursing schools and the nursing profession, in general, to support nurses through education and with rehabilitation.[13]

Research has repeatedly shown the importance of identifying signs and symptoms of substance use and abuse, suggesting that it be acknowledged with systems in place for prevention and intervention. When nurses have easy access to drugs, increasing job stress, and a personal family history of substance abuse, they have the highest risks for substance use disorders.[14] A lack of preparedness about substance use and abuse in the profession may result in individuals not intervening in performance problems suspected to be related to a substance use disorder. This fosters unsafe conditions when colleagues make excuses, ignore problems, cover up mistakes, and accept incomplete work.[15]

NOTES

1. M. Buckner, "Substance Abuse among Nursing Students," Dean's Notes 23, no. 3 (2002); L. Bugle et al., "Attitudes of Nursing Faculty Regarding Students with a Chemical Dependency: A National Survey," Journal of Addictions Nursing 14, no. 3 (2003); M. Haack and T. Harford, "Drinking Patterns among Student Nurses," The International Journal of the Addictions 19 (1984); K. Kornegay et al., "Facing a Problem of Great Concern: Nursing Faculty's Lived Experience of Encounters with Chemically Dependent Nursing Students," Journal of Addictions Nursing 15, no. 3 (2004).

2. Buckner, "Substance Abuse among Nursing Students."; Bugle et al., "Attitudes of Nursing Faculty Regarding Students with a Chemical Dependency: A National Survey."; E. Coleman et al., "Assessing Substance Abuse among Health Care Students and the Efficacy of Educational Interventions," Journal of Professional Nursing 13, no. 1 (1997).

3. P. Zickler, "Nida Scientific Panel Reports on Prescription Drug Misuse and Abuse," National Institute on Drug Abuse Notes 16, no. 3 (2001).

4. National Institute on Drug Abuse (NIDA), Drug Abuse and Addiction: The Basics, (2016), http://www.drugabuse.gov/publications/media-guide/science-drug-abuse-addiction-basics.

5. R. Martinez, "Innovative Roles Executive Director of Peer Assistance Services: An Interview with Elizabeth M. Pace," Journal of Addictions Nursing 13, no. 1 (2001); Zickler, "Nida Scientific Panel Reports on Prescription Drug Misuse and Abuse."

6. T. B. Monroe, "Addressing Substance Misuse among Nursing Student: Development of a Prototype Alternative-to-Dismissal Policy," Journal of Nursing Education 8 (2009).

7. D. Murphy-Parker and R. J. Martinez, "Nursing Students' Personal Experiences Involving Alcohol Problems," Archives of Psychiatric Nursing 19, no. 3 (2005).

8. M. O. Howard et al., "Alcohol and Drug Education in Schools of Nursing," Journal of Alcohol and Drug Education 42, no. 3 (1997).

9. D. M. Cadiz et al., "Quasi-Experimental Evaluation of a Substance Use Awareness Educational Intervention for Nursing Students," Nurse Education 51 (2012); T. Monroe and F. Pearson, "Treating Nurses and Student Nurses with Chemical Dependency: Revising Policy in

the United States for the 21st Century," International Journal of Mental Health and Addiction 7 (2009); Murphy-Parker and Martinez, "Nursing Students' Personal Experiences Involving Alcohol Problems."; National Student Nurses Association (NSNA), "Resolution: In Support of Nursing School Policies to Assist and Advocate for Nursing Students Experiencing Impaired Practice," in National Student Nurses Association (Philadelphia, PA: NSNA House of Delegates, 2002); D. Quinlan, "Impaired Nursing Practice: A National Perspective on Peer Assistance in the U.S.," Journal of Addictions Nursing 14, no. 149–155 (2003); G. H. Rassool, "Curriculum Model, Course Development, and Evaluation of Substance Misuse Education for Health Care Professionals," ibid.15, no. 85–90 (2004); G. H. Rassool and S. Rawaf, "Predictors of Educational Outcomes of Undergraduate Nursing Students in Alcohol and Drug Education," Nurse Education Today 28 (2008).

10. Cadiz et al., "Quasi-Experimental Evaluation of a Substance Use Awareness Educational Intervention for Nursing Students."

11. Ibid.

12. Kornegay et al., "Facing a Problem of Great Concern: Nursing Faculty's Lived Experience of Encounters with Chemically Dependent Nursing Students."

13. Monroe and Pearson, "Treating Nurses and Student Nurses with Chemical Dependency: Revising Policy in the United States for the 21st Century."

14. G. A. Kenna and M. D. Wood, "Family History of Alcohol and Drug Use in Healthcare Professionals," Journal of Substance Use 10 (2005); G. Monahan, "Drug Use/Misuse among Health Professionals," Substance Use & Misuse 38 (2003); M. M. West, "Early Risk Indicators of Substance Abuse among Nurses," Journal of Nursing Scholarship 34, no. 2 (2002).

15. Quinlan, "Impaired Nursing Practice: A National Perspective on Peer Assistance in the U.S.."

BIBLIOGRAPHY

Buckner, M. "Substance Abuse among Nursing Students." *Dean's Notes* 23, no. 3 (2002): 1.

Bugle, L., F. Jackson, K. Kornegay, and K. Rives. "Attitudes of Nursing Faculty Regarding Students with a Chemical Dependency: A National Survey." *Journal of Addictions Nursing* 14, no. 3 (2003): 125–32.

Cadiz, D. M., C. O'Neill, S. S. Butell, B. J. Epeneter, and B. Basin. "Quasi-Experimental Evaluation of a Substance Use Awareness Educational Intervention for Nursing Students." *Nurse Education* 51 (2012): 411–15.

Coleman, E., G. Honeycutt, B. Ogden, D. McMillian, P. O'Sullivan, K. Light, and W. Wingfield. "Assessing Substance Abuse among Health Care Students and the Efficacy of Educational Interventions." *Journal of Professional Nursing* 13, no. 1 (1997): 28–37.

Haack, M., and T. Harford. "Drinking Patterns among Student Nurses." *The International Journal of the Addictions* 19 (1984): 577–83.

Howard, M. O., R. D. Walker, P. S. Walker, and R. T. Suchinsky. "Alcohol and Drug Education in Schools of Nursing." *Journal of Alcohol and Drug Education* 42, no. 3 (1997): 54–80.

Kenna, G. A., and M. D. Wood. "Family History of Alcohol and Drug Use in Healthcare Professionals." *Journal of Substance Use* 10 (2005): 225–38.

Kornegay, K., L. Bugle, E. Jackson, and K. Rives. "Facing a Problem of Great Concern: Nursing Faculty's Lived Experience of Encounters with Chemically Dependent Nursing Students." *Journal of Addictions Nursing* 15, no. 3 (2004): 125–32.

Martinez, R. "Innovative Roles Executive Director of Peer Assistance Services: An Interview with Elizabeth M. Pace." *Journal of Addictions Nursing* 13, no. 1 (2001): 49–51.

Monahan, G. "Drug Use/Misuse among Health Professionals." *Substance Use & Misuse* 38 (2003): 1877–81.

Monroe, T. B. "Addressing Substance Misuse among Nursing Student: Development of a Prototype Alternative-to-Dismissal Policy." *Journal of Nursing Education* 8 (2009): 272–77.

Monroe, T., and F. Pearson. "Treating Nurses and Student Nurses with Chemical Dependency: Revising Policy in the United States for the 21st Century." *International Journal of Mental Health and Addiction* 7 (2009): 530–40.

Murphy-Parker, D., and R. J. Martinez. "Nursing Students' Personal Experiences Involving Alcohol Problems." *Archives of Psychiatric Nursing* 19, no. 3 (2005): 150–58.

National Institute on Drug Abuse (NIDA). *Drug Abuse and Addiction: The Basics*. 2016. http://www.drugabuse.gov/publications/media-guide/science-drug-abuse-addiction-basics.

National Student Nurses Association (NSNA). "Resolution: In Support of Nursing School Policies to Assist and Advocate for Nursing Students Experiencing Impaired Practice." In *National Student Nurses Association* Philadelphia, PA: NSNA House of Delegates, 2002.

Quinlan, D. "Impaired Nursing Practice: A National Perspective on Peer Assistance in the U.S." *Journal of Addictions Nursing* 14, no. 149–155 (2003).

Rassool, G. H. "Curriculum Model, Course Development, and Evaluation of Substance Misuse Education for Health Care Professionals." *Journal of Addictions Nursing* 15, no. 85–90 (2004).

Rassool, G. H., and S. Rawaf. "Predictors of Educational Outcomes of Undergraduate Nursing Students in Alcohol and Drug Education." *Nurse Education Today* 28 (2008): 691–701.

West, M. M. "Early Risk Indicators of Substance Abuse among Nurses." *Journal of Nursing Scholarship* 34, no. 2 (2002): 187–93.

Zickler, P. "Nida Scientific Panel Reports on Prescription Drug Misuse and Abuse." *National Institute on Drug Abuse Notes* 16, no. 3 (2001): 1–5.

III

NURSES AND RECOVERY

"I found out that I had no vote as to whether or not I was going to be an alcoholic—no vote. What I had a vote in was whether I was going to do recovery so that's where my energy went . . . Recovery is a gift"

—Heather

Chapter Seven

Nurses in Recovery

Numerous studies have emphasized the prevalence of substance use disorders in the nursing profession; however, there is little known about nurses in recovery.[1] Barriers for treatment and eventual recovery for nurses have been caused by a lack of education and information regarding substance use disorders.[2] Additionally, those in the medical profession, and particularly in nursing, are more severely punitive towards their colleagues who suffer from substance use disorders than towards the general public.[3] Ineffective and punitive policies make it difficult for both nurses and nursing students to seek treatment.[4]

IDENTIFICATION AND INTERVENTION

Early identification, intervention, and monitoring of nurses with substance use disorders provide the greatest protection for patients, as well as best outcomes for nurses in recovery.[5] Identifying and addressing a substance use disorder in a nurse and acknowledging the denial in the healthcare setting surrounding the nurse can be difficult;[6] however, it is in these healthcare settings where most referrals to treatment do occur.[7]

Research has shown that the earlier a substance abuse problem is recognized and addressed, the better the chances for rehabilitation and recovery.[8] Several studies have indicated that a positive attitude, education, and early intervention can improve the eventual outcome for nurses with substance use disorders.[9] Intervention is crucial as a first step in assisting nurses with substance use disorders to willingly enter into treatment. An intervention can be one of life's most traumatic events, for both those doing the intervening as well as the suspected substance abuser, therefore, it should be done with preparation and rational support.[10]

A public health policy that identifies screening, brief intervention and referral to treatment (SBIRT) is showing a lot of potential related to earlier recognition, identification, and referral to treatment.[11] It provides early identification and intervention for many with chronic medical problems.[12] SBIRT has been modified for at-risk alcohol and substance abuse programs. It has been successful as an instrument in many of the nurse programs.[13]

There needs to be further research in primary care settings that focus on the development of new instruments that screen and suggest treatment and referral systems. This should be done in conjunction with developing targeted prevention and treatment programs.[14] It is important to identify early risk factors so targeted early intervention and prevention strategies can be developed to tackle the issues of substance abuse within the nurse profession.[15]

NOTES

1. D. H. Angres, K. Bettinardi-Angres, and W. Cross, "Nurses with Chemical Dependency: Promoting Successful Treatment and Reentry," Journal of Nursing Regulation 1, no. 1 (2010); D. Dunn, "Substance Abuse among Nurses – Intercession and Intervention," Association of Operating Room Nurses Journal 82, no. 2 (2005); P. D. Hart, "Faces and Voices of Recovery Public Survey," (Washington, DC: Peter D. Hart Research Associates, 2004); B. Heise, "The Historical Context of Addiction in the Nursing Profession: 1850-1982," Journal of Addictions Nurse 14, no. 3 (2003); A. B. Laudet, "What Does Recovery Mean to You? Lessons from the Recovery Experience for Research and Practice," Journal of Substance Abuse Treatment 33 (2007); A. M. McNelis et al., "Indiana State Nurses Assistance Program: Identifying Gender Differences in Substance Use Disorders," Perspectives in Psychiatric Care 48, no. 1 (2012); M. A. Naegle, "Drug and Alcohol Abuse in Nursing," Nursing Life 8, no. 1 (1988); Substance Abuse and Mental Health Services Administration (SAMHSA), "Results from the 2006 National Survey on Drug Use and Health: National Findings," (Rockville, MD: Office of Applied Studies, 2007); A. M. Trinkoff and C. L. Storr, "Substance Use among Nurses: Differences between Specialties," American Journal of Public Health 88 (1998a); A. M. Trinkoff, C. L. Storr, and M. P. Wall, "Prescription-Type Drug Misuse and Workplace Access among Nurses," Journal of Addictive Diseases 18, no. 1 (1999).

2. D. M. Cadiz et al., "Quasi-Experimental Evaluation of a Substance Use Awareness Educational Intervention for Nursing Students," Nurse Education 51 (2012); T. Hughes and E. Sullivan, "Attitudes toward Chemically Dependent Nurses: Care or Curse?," in Addiction in the Nursing Profession ed. M. R. Haack and T. L. Hughes (New York: Springer, 1989); H. Lippman and S. Nagle, "Addicted Nurses: Tolerated, Tormented, or Treated?," Nursing Forum 55, no. 4 (1992); D. Quinlan, "Impaired Nursing Practice: A National Perspective on Peer Assistance in the U.S.," Journal of Addictions Nursing 14, no. 149–155 (2003); P. A. Wennerstorm and L. A. Rooda, "Attitudes and Perceptions of Nursing Students toward Chemically Impaired Nurses: Implications for Nursing Education," Journal of Nursing Education 35 (1996).

3. M. McHugh, K. Papastrat, and J. Ashton, "Assessing the Drug Addicted Nurse: Information for the Legal Nurse Consultant," Journal of Legal Nurse Consulting 22, no. 3 (2011).

4. T. B. Monroe and H. Kenaga, "Don't Ask Don't Tell: Substance Abuse and Addiction among Nurses," Journal of Clinical Nursing 20 (2010).

5. Susanne Astrab Fogger and Teena McGuinness, "Alabama's Nurse Monitoring Programs: The Nurse's Experience of Being Monitored," Journal of Addictions Nursing 20, no. 3 (2009); M. Haack and C. Yocom, "State Policies and Nurses with Substance Use Disorders," Journal of Nursing Scholarship 34, no. 1 (2002).

6. L. Hanks and L. Bissell, "Health Professionals," in Substance Abuse: A Comprehensive Textbook, ed. J. H. Lowinson, P. Ruiz, and R. B. Milkman (Philadelphia, PA: Lippincott, Williams & Wilkins, 1992); National Council of State Boards of Nursing (NCSBN), "Substance Use Disorder in Nursing, a Resource Manual and Guidelines for Alternative and Disciplinary Monitoring Programs," (2011), https://www.ncsbn.org/SUDN_11.pdf.

7. L. Duke and H. Zsobar, "Monitoring Nurses with License Probation" (paper presented at the National Council of State Boards of Nursing Annual Meeting, St. Louis, MO, 1995); M. Kelly and S. Mynatt, "Addiction among Nurses: Does the Health Care Industry Compound the Problem?," Health Care Management Review 15, no. 4 (1990); L. Smith, B. B. Taylor, and T. L. Hughes, "Effective Peer Responses to Impaired Nursing Practice," Nursing Clinics of North America 33, no. 1 (1998); D. G. Talbot and P. Wilson, "Physicians and Other Health Professionals," in Substance Abuse: A Comprehensive Textbook, ed. J. H. Lowinson, et al. (Philadelphia, PA: Lippincott, Williams & Wilkins, 2005).

8. R. A. Eller and B. L. Irwin, "Responding to the Chemically Dependent Nursing Student," Journal of Nursing Education 28, no. 2 (1989); G. E. LaGodna and M. J. Hendrix, "Impaired Nurses: A Cost Analysis," JONA: The Journal of Nursing Administration 19, no. 9 (1989); National Council of State Boards of Nursing (NCSBN), "Substance Use Disorder in Nursing, a Resource Manual and Guidelines for Alternative and Disciplinary Monitoring Programs."

9. C. Clark and J. Farnsworth, "Program for Recovering Nurses: An Evaluation," Medical Surgery Nursing 14 (2006); L. M. Cook, "Can Nurses Trust Nurses in Recovery Reentering the Workplace?" Nursing Clinics of North America 43, no. 3 (2013); Monroe and Kenaga, "Don't Ask Don't Tell: Substance Abuse and Addiction among Nurses;" L. M. Pullen and L. A. Green, "Identification, Intervention and Education: Essential Curriculum Components for Chemical Dependency in Nurses," The Journal of Continuing Education in Nursing 28 (1997).

10. R. H. Coombs, Drug-Impaired Professionals (Cambridge, MA: Harvard University Press, 1997).

11. National Council of State Boards of Nursing (NCSBN), "Substance Use Disorder in Nursing, a Resource Manual and Guidelines for Alternative and Disciplinary Monitoring Programs;" E. Tighe and L. Saxe, "Community-Based Substance Abuse Reduction and the Gap between Treatment Need and Treatment Utilization: Analysis of Data from the "Fighting Back" General Population Survey," Journal of Drug Issues 36, no. 2 (2006).

12. Office of National Drug Control Policy & Substance Abuse and Mental Health Services Administration, Fact Sheet: Screening, Brief Intervention, and Referral to Treatment (Sbirt), (2012), http://www.whitehouse.gov/sites/default/files/page/files/sbirt_fact_sheet_ondcp-samh-sa_7-25-111.pdf; K. Puskar et al., "Faculty Buy-in to Teach Alcohol and Drug Use Screening," Journal of Continuing Education in Nursing 45 (2014); Substance Abuse and Mental Health Services Administration (SAMHSA), "Results from the 2012 National Survey on Drug Use and Health: Summary of National Findings " (Rockville, MD: Substance Abuse and Mental Health Services Administration, 2013).

13. National Council of State Boards of Nursing (NCSBN), "Substance Use Disorder in Nursing, a Resource Manual and Guidelines for Alternative and Disciplinary Monitoring Programs."

14. D. Carise et al., "Getting Patients the Services They Need Using a Computer-Assisted System for Patient Assessment and Referral: Caspar," Drug Alcohol Dependency 80 (2005).

15. D. Snow and T. Hughes, "Prevalence of Alcohol and Other Drug Use and Abuse among Nurses," Journal of Addictions Nursing 14, no. 3 (2003).

BIBLIOGRAPHY

Angres, D. H., K. Bettinardi-Angres, and W. Cross. "Nurses with Chemical Dependency: Promoting Successful Treatment and Reentry." *Journal of Nursing Regulation* 1, no. 1 (2010): 16–20.

Cadiz, D. M., C. O'Neill, S. S. Butell, B. J. Epeneter, and B. Basin. "Quasi-Experimental Evaluation of a Substance Use Awareness Educational Intervention for Nursing Students." *Nurse Education* 51 (2012): 411–15.

Carise, D., O. Gurel, A. T. McLellan, K. Dugosh, and C. Kendig. "Getting Patients the Services They Need Using a Computer-Assisted System for Patient Assessment and Referral: Caspar." *Drug Alcohol Dependency* 80 (2005): 177–89.

Clark, C., and J. Farnsworth. "Program for Recovering Nurses: An Evaluation." *Medical Surgery Nursing* 14 (2006): 223–30.

Cook, L. M. "Can Nurses Trust Nurses in Recovery Reentering the Workplace?" *Nursing Clinics of North America* 43, no. 3 (2013): 21–24.

Coombs, R. H. *Drug-Impaired Professionals.* Cambridge, MA: Harvard University Press, 1997.

Duke, L., and H. Zsobar. "Monitoring Nurses with License Probation." Paper presented at the National Council of State Boards of Nursing Annual Meeting, St. Louis, MO, 1995.

Dunn, D. "Substance Abuse among Nurses–Intercession and Intervention." *Association of Operating Room Nurses Journal* 82, no. 2 (2005): 87–88.

Eller, R. A., and B. L. Irwin. "Responding to the Chemically Dependent Nursing Student." *Journal of Nursing Education* 28, no. 2 (1989): 87–88.

Fogger, Susanne Astrab, and Teena McGuinness. "Alabama's Nurse Monitoring Programs: The Nurse's Experience of Being Monitored." *Journal of Addictions Nursing* 20, no. 3 (2009/01/01 2009): 142–49.

Haack, M., and C. Yocom. "State Policies and Nurses with Substance Use Disorders." *Journal of Nursing Scholarship* 34, no. 1 (2002): 89–94.

Hanks, L., and L. Bissell. "Health Professionals." In *Substance Abuse: A Comprehensive Textbook*, edited by J. H. Lowinson, P. Ruiz and R. B. Milkman. Philadelphia, PA: Lippincott, Williams & Wilkins, 1992.

Hart, P. D. "Faces and Voices of Recovery Public Survey." Washington, DC: Peter D. Hart Research Associates, 2004.

Heise, B. "The Historical Context of Addiction in the Nursing Profession: 1850-1982." *Journal of Addictions Nurse* 14, no. 3 (2003): 117–24.

Hughes, T., and E. Sullivan. "Attitudes toward Chemically Dependent Nurses: Care or Curse?" In *Addiction in the Nursing Profession* edited by M. R. Haack and T. L. Hughes. New York: Springer, 1989.

Kelly, M., and S. Mynatt. "Addiction among Nurses: Does the Health Care Industry Compound the Problem?" *Health Care Management Review* 15, no. 4 (1990): 35–42.

LaGodna, G. E., and M. J. Hendrix. "Impaired Nurses: A Cost Analysis." *JONA: The Journal of Nursing Administration* 19, no. 9 (1989): 13–18.

Laudet, A. B. "What Does Recovery Mean to You? Lessons from the Recovery Experience for Research and Practice." *Journal of Substance Abuse Treatment* 33 (2007): 243–56.

Lippman, H., and S. Nagle. "Addicted Nurses: Tolerated, Tormented, or Treated?" *Nursing Forum* 55, no. 4 (1992): 36–42.

McHugh, M., K. Papastrat, and J. Ashton. "Assessing the Drug Addicted Nurse: Information for the Legal Nurse Consultant." *Journal of Legal Nurse Consulting* 22, no. 3 (2011): 11–14.

McNelis, A. M., S. Horton-Deutsch, P. O'Haver Day, T. Gavardinas, C. Outlaw, R. Palmer, and M. Schroeder. "Indiana State Nurses Assistance Program: Identifying Gender Differences in Substance Use Disorders." *Perspectives in Psychiatric Care* 48, no. 1 (2012): 41–46.

Monroe, T. B., and H. Kenaga. "Don't Ask Don't Tell: Substance Abuse and Addiction among Nurses." *Journal of Clinical Nursing* 20 (2010): 504–09.

Naegle, M. A. "Drug and Alcohol Abuse in Nursing." *Nursing Life* 8, no. 1 (1988): 42.54.

National Council of State Boards of Nursing (NCSBN). "Substance Use Disorder in Nursing, a Resource Manual and Guidelines for Alternative and Disciplinary Monitoring Programs." (2011): 280. https://www.ncsbn.org/SUDN_11.pdf.

Office of National Drug Control Policy & Substance Abuse and Mental Health Services Administration. *Fact Sheet: Screening, Brief Intervention, and Referral to Treatment (Sbirt).*

2012. http://www.whitehouse.gov/sites/default/files/page/files/sbirt_fact_sheet_ondcp-samhsa_7-25-111.pdf.

Pullen, L. M., and L. A. Green. "Identification, Intervention and Education: Essential Curriculum Components for Chemical Dependency in Nurses." *The Journal of Continuing Education in Nursing* 28 (1997): 211–16.

Puskar, K., A. M. Mitchell, I. Kane, H. Hagle, and K. S. Talcott. "Faculty Buy-in to Teach Alcohol and Drug Use Screening." *Journal of Continuing Education in Nursing* 45 (2014): 403–08.

Quinlan, D. "Impaired Nursing Practice: A National Perspective on Peer Assistance in the U.S." *Journal of Addictions Nursing* 14, no. 149–155 (2003).

Smith, L., B. B. Taylor, and T. L. Hughes. "Effective Peer Responses to Impaired Nursing Practice." *Nursing Clinics of North America* 33, no. 1 (1998): 105–18.

Snow, D., and T. Hughes. "Prevalence of Alcohol and Other Drug Use and Abuse among Nurses." *Journal of Addictions Nursing* 14, no. 3 (2003): 165–67.

Substance Abuse and Mental Health Services Administration (SAMHSA). "Results from the 2006 National Survey on Drug Use and Health: National Findings." Rockville, MD: Office of Applied Studies, 2007.

———. "Results from the 2012 National Survey on Drug Use and Health: Summary of National Findings." Rockville, MD: Substance Abuse and Mental Health Services Administration, 2013.

Talbot, D. G., and P. Wilson. "Physicians and Other Health Professionals." In *Substance Abuse: A Comprehensive Textbook*, edited by J. H. Lowinson, P. Ruiz, R. B. Millman and J. G. Langrod, 1187-202. Philadelphia, PA: Lippincott, Williams & Wilkins, 2005.

Tighe, E., and L. Saxe. "Community-Based Substance Abuse Reduction and the Gap between Treatment Need and Treatment Utilization: Analysis of Data from the "Fighting Back" General Population Survey." *Journal of Drug Issues* 36, no. 2 (2006): 165–86.

Trinkoff, A. M., and C. L. Storr. "Substance Use among Nurses: Differences between Specialties." *American Journal of Public Health* 88 (1998a): 581–86.

Trinkoff, A. M., C. L. Storr, and M. P. Wall. "Prescription-Type Drug Misuse and Workplace Access among Nurses." *Journal of Addictive Diseases* 18, no. 1 (1999): 9–16.

Wennerstorm, P. A., and L. A. Rooda. "Attitudes and Perceptions of Nursing Students toward Chemically Impaired Nurses: Implications for Nursing Education." *Journal of Nursing Education* 35 (1996): 237–39.

Chapter Eight

Successful Support and Recovery Systems

Support systems established within the nursing profession are essential for providing nurses with the fundamental treatment, care, and assistance needed for them to succeed in recovery. An example of a successful support system for nurses and other healthcare professionals has been the alternative to discipline programs.[1] These programs were developed in the 1970s and 1980s in response to the widespread acknowledgment and prevalence of substance use disorders among registered nurses and the lack of treatment afforded nurses with the disease.[2] Alternatives to discipline programs are comprehensive monitoring programs that place RNs into a structured plan of treatment.[3]

Several different models are used in these programs throughout the United States. They include a combination of the peer support and assistance to treatment along with the customary disciplinary model.[4] They provide Boards of Nursing with the ability to identify substance use disorders in a nurse's practice earlier and intervene in a manner that provides greater public protection.[5] Before the introduction of alternatives to discipline programs, drug use and substance use disorders in the healthcare industry were addressed punitively. Healthcare professionals with substance use disorders had to be jailed, their licenses revoked, and their careers destroyed.[6] The lengthy time-consuming disciplinary approach had been the only way to remove nurses and others from practice and protect the public from unsafe care.[7]

The National Organization of Alternative Programs (NOAP) was created in 1999 to provide quality alternatives to discipline programs for nurses with substance use disorders regardless of their geographic location.[8] In 2002, the ANA adopted a resolution that encouraged the development and use of these alternatives to discipline programs for health professionals in those states where they did not exist.[9] The ANA also advocated for nursing students to be included in these programs; however, most of the programs across the United States still do not monitor substance use disorders among students.[10]

These support peer assistance programs prevent nurses' licenses from being suspended or revoked and monitor the nurses' return to work.[11] Research indicates that these types of programs are better able to retain nurses, support them into recovery, and return them to practice.[12] In one of the few studies of relapse rates for nurses enrolled in alternatives to discipline programs, nurses in these programs had only a 41.7% relapse rate as compared to the 75% relapse rate for the general public.[13] The program models that have the right combination of treatment support, such as long-term treatment, aftercare, sanctions, and monitoring, have proven to be the most effective.[14] The end result of effective treatment is recovery.

RECOVERY EXPOUNDED

Recovery is a difficult term to define as there are various definitions with nothing universally accepted.[15] It is described more as "personal development and a lifestyle and that includes outlook, abstinence, liberation from your compulsion, and a return to more mental, physical, and emotional well-being."[16] NCSBN[17] indicates there are three foundational elements to recovery. First is identifying the life-threatening aspect of substance abuse. Second is maintaining abstinence. Third is developing the support programs to maintain sobriety.[18] SAMHSA described recovery as a process wherein one strives to reach their utmost potential.[19] McLellan et al. noted that recovery is evidenced by "reduction in substance use, improvements in personal and social health, and reduction in threats to public health and safety."[20] Millar and Stermac described that important factors identified in recovery processes for women have included "strategies to address affect regulation; development of a new self-concept; and the forging of more adaptive attachment styles."[21]

Recovery may take on many forms and behaviors, and it is more than just the absence of use.[22] It is being reconnected to healthier behaviors and relationships and detached from alcohol and drugs.[23] This reconnection is an important part of self-acceptance, self-care, and coping.[24] Additionally, other researchers declare that recovery is a lifestyle change and is the process by which the substance use disorder is recognized as problematic and avoided.[25] This is especially needed, as research indicates many individuals susceptible to substance use disorders also have many other risk factors.[26] To be successful in recovery, the risk factors need to be identified and acknowledged. Regardless of how recovery is described, it is the goal of nurses who enter into treatment to overcome their substance use disorders.

Recovery is vital to the health of society.[27] It is considered a gift by those nurses who have experienced the devastation of drug addiction and its consequences. Recovery requires a lifestyle change and is a lifelong process. Early identification and education along with established support systems have been suggested as ways to support recovery and improve the outcomes of nurses dealing with substance use disorders, as well as to protect employers and the public from the care of impaired nurses.[28]

Those who seek treatment are estimated to have a higher satisfaction of life.[29] Nurses respond well to substance abuse treatment with up to 70% successfully returning to practice.[30] The stories of those nurses whose lives have been changed by treatment and support and who are now living a life of successful recovery are rarely told.[31] Most studies have researched the public's views of substance misuse and abuse but have done very little examination regarding the public's opinion regarding recovery.[32] These stories are the ones that need to be emphasized and shared to let others know recovery is possible.

A nurse in recovery is more than an individual who has abstained from use. It is a nurse who has experienced behavioral and lifestyle changes and has become attached to improved and healthier associations.[33] Such a change should be the ultimate objective of nurses entering into treatment.[34] Additionally, providing an avenue for nurses to enter into treatment and recovery should also be an important goal of the nursing profession. The importance and possibility of recovery for those nurses suffering from substance use disorders should be emphasized. The stories describing these changes need to be shared with others to help support a flourishing healthy nursing community and society. Recovery community support is vital, as it provides the connections and lifestyle change needed to enable a nurse to maintain his or her sobriety and develop into a healthy, productive member of the healthcare community.

NOTES

1. T. B. Monroe and H. Kenaga, "Don't Ask Don't Tell: Substance Abuse and Addiction among Nurses," Journal of Clinical Nursing 20 (2010).

2. Ibid.; National Council of State Boards of Nursing (NCSBN), "Substance Use Disorder in Nursing, a Resource Manual and Guidelines for Alternative and Disciplinary Monitoring Programs," (2011), https://www.ncsbn.org/SUDN_11.pdf.

3. C. Clark and J. Farnsworth, "Program for Recovering Nurses: An Evaluation," Medical Surgery Nursing 14 (2006); D. Quinlan, "Impaired Nursing Practice: A National Perspective on Peer Assistance in the U.S.," Journal of Addictions Nursing 14, no. 149–155 (2003).

4. National Council of State Boards of Nursing (NCSBN), "Substance Use Disorder in Nursing, a Resource Manual and Guidelines for Alternative and Disciplinary Monitoring Programs."

5. Ibid.; E. Sullivan and P. Decker, Effective Leadership and Management in Nursing (Upper Saddle River, NJ: Prentice Hall, 2001); C. Yocom and M. Haack, Interim Report: A

Comparison of Two Regulatory Approaches to the Management of the Chemically Dependent Nurse (Chicago, IL: National Council of State Boards of Nursing, 1996).

6. B. Heise, "The Historical Context of Addiction in the Nursing Profession: 1850–1982," Journal of Addictions Nurse 14, no. 3 (2003); National Council of State Boards of Nursing (NCSBN), "Substance Use Disorder in Nursing, a Resource Manual and Guidelines for Alternative and Disciplinary Monitoring Programs."

7. "Substance Use Disorder in Nursing, a Resource Manual and Guidelines for Alternative and Disciplinary Monitoring Programs."

8. As cited in Quinlan, "Impaired Nursing Practice: A National Perspective on Peer Assistance in the U.S.."

9. Ibid.

10. National Council of State Boards of Nursing (NCSBN), "Substance Use Disorder in Nursing, a Resource Manual and Guidelines for Alternative and Disciplinary Monitoring Programs."

11. Clark and Farnsworth, "Program for Recovering Nurses: An Evaluation."

12. M. Haack and C. Yocom, "State Policies and Nurses with Substance Use Disorders," Journal of Nursing Scholarship 34, no. 1 (2002); L. J. Merlo and M. S. Gold, "Addiction Research and Treatment: The State of the Art in 2008," Psychiatric Times 25, no. 7 (2008); National Council of State Boards of Nursing (NCSBN), "Substance Use Disorder in Nursing, a Resource Manual and Guidelines for Alternative and Disciplinary Monitoring Programs;" Quinlan, "Impaired Nursing Practice: A National Perspective on Peer Assistance in the U.S.."

13. L. Baldwin and V. Smith, "Relapse in Chemically Dependent Nurses: Prevalence and Contributing Factors," Issue: Newsletter of the National Council 15, no. 1 (1994).

14. A. T. McLellan et al., "Five Year Outcomes in a Cohort Study of Physicians Treated for Substance Use Disorders in the United States," British Medical Journal 337 (2008); Merlo and Gold, "Addiction Research and Treatment: The State of the Art in 2008."

15. K. Crowley and C. Morgan, Re/Entry: A Guide for Nurses Dealing with Substance Use Disorder (Indianapolis, IN: Sigma Theta Tau International, 2014).

16. Ibid., 19.

17. National Council of State Boards of Nursing (NCSBN), "Substance Use Disorder in Nursing, a Resource Manual and Guidelines for Alternative and Disciplinary Monitoring Programs."

18. J. F. Kelly et al., "A 3-Year Study of Addiction Mutual-Help Group Participation Following Intensive Outpatient Treatment," Alcoholism: Clinical and Experimental Research 30 (2006); M. J. Landry, Understanding Drugs of Abuse: The Processes of Addiction, Treatment and Recovery (Washington, DC: American Psychiatric Press, 1994).

19. S. L. Hedden, "Behavioral Health Trends in the United States: Results from the 2014 National Survey on Drug Use and Health," (2015). http://www.samhsa.gov/data/sites/default/files/NSDUH-FRR1-2014/NSDUH-FRR1-2014.pdf

20. A. T. McLellan et al., "Reconsidering the Evaluation of Addiction Treatment: From Retrospective Follow-up to Concurrent Recovery Monitoring," Addiction 100 (2005): 448.

21. G. Millar and L. Stermac, "Substance Abuse and Childhood Maltreatment," The American Journal on Addictions 22, no. 6 (2000): 178.

22. J. Blomqvist, "Recovery with and without Treatment: A Comparison of Resolutions of Alcohol and Drug Problems," Addiction Research & Theory 10, no. 2 (2002); R. Margolis, A. Kilpatrick, and B. Mooney, "A Retrospective Look at Long-Term Adolescent Recovery: Clinicians Talk to Researchers," Journal of Psychoactive Drugs 32, no. 1 (2000).

23. C. Masters and D. S. Carlson, "The Process of Reconnecting: Recovery from the Perspective of Addicted Women," Journal of Addictions Nursing 17 (2006).

24. L. G. Payne, "Self-Acceptance and Its Role in Women's Recovery from Addiction," ibid.21 (2010).

25. A. B. Laudet, "What Does Recovery Mean to You? Lessons from the Recovery Experience for Research and Practice," Journal of Substance Abuse Treatment 33 (2007).

26. M. M. West, "Early Risk Indicators of Substance Abuse among Nurses," Journal of Nursing Scholarship 34, no. 2 (2002).

27. M. Hansen, B. Ganley, and C. Carlucci, "Journeys from Addiction to Recovery," Research and Theory for Nursing Practice 22 (2008); S. Horton-Deutsch, A. McNelis, and P. O'Haver Day, "Enhancing Mutual Accountability to Promote Quality, Safety, and Nurses' Recovery from Substance Use Disorders," Archives of Psychiatric Nursing 25 (2011); Laudet, "What Does Recovery Mean to You? Lessons from the Recovery Experience for Research and Practice;" S. Srivastava and M. S. Bhatia, "Quality of Life as an Outcome Measure in the Treatment of Alcohol Dependence," Industrial Psychiatry Journal 22, no. 1 (2013).

28. N. Darbro, "Alternative Diversion Programs for Nurses with Impaired Practice: Completers and Non-Completers," Journal of Addictions Nursing 16, no. 4 (2005); G. H. Rassool and S. Rawaf, "Predictors of Educational Outcomes of Undergraduate Nursing Students in Alcohol and Drug Education," Nurse Education Today 28 (2008).

29. Laudet, "What Does Recovery Mean to You? Lessons from the Recovery Experience for Research and Practice;" A. B. Laudet, J. B. Becker, and W. L. White, "Don't Wanna Go through That Madness No More: Quality of Life Satisfaction as Predictor of Sustained Remission from Illicit Drug Misuse," Substance Use & Misuse 44 (2009); Srivastava and Bhatia, "Quality of Life as an Outcome Measure in the Treatment of Alcohol Dependence."

30. L. J. Young, "Education for Worksite Monitors of Impaired Nurses," Nurse Administration Quarterly 32, no. 4 (2008).

31. D. H. Angres, K. Bettinardi-Angres, and W. Cross, "Nurses with Chemical Dependency: Promoting Successful Treatment and Reentry," Journal of Nursing Regulation 1, no. 1 (2010); P. D. Hart, "Faces and Voices of Recovery Public Survey," (Washington, DC: Peter D. Hart Research Associates, 2004); Laudet, "What Does Recovery Mean to You? Lessons from the Recovery Experience for Research and Practice."

32. Hart, "Faces and Voices of Recovery Public Survey."

33. Laudet, "What Does Recovery Mean to You? Lessons from the Recovery Experience for Research and Practice;" Masters and Carlson, "The Process of Reconnecting: Recovery from the Perspective of Addicted Women."

34. "The Process of Reconnecting: Recovery from the Perspective of Addicted Women."

BIBLIOGRAPHY

Angres, D. H., K. Bettinardi-Angres, and W. Cross. "Nurses with Chemical Dependency: Promoting Successful Treatment and Reentry." *Journal of Nursing Regulation* 1, no. 1 (2010): 16–20.

Baldwin, L., and V. Smith. "Relapse in Chemically Dependent Nurses: Prevalence and Contributing Factors." *Issue: Newsletter of the National Council* 15, no. 1 (1994): 1–9.

Blomqvist, J. "Recovery with and without Treatment: A Comparison of Resolutions of Alcohol and Drug Problems." *Addiction Research & Theory* 10, no. 2 (2002): 119–58.

Clark, C., and J. Farnsworth. "Program for Recovering Nurses: An Evaluation." *Medical Surgery Nursing* 14 (2006): 223–30.

Crowley, K., and C. Morgan. *Re/Entry: A Guide for Nurses Dealing with Substance Use Disorder.* Indianapolis, IN: Sigma Theta Tau International, 2014.

Darbro, N. "Alternative Diversion Programs for Nurses with Impaired Practice: Completers and Non-Completers." *Journal of Addictions Nursing* 16, no. 4 (2005): 169–86.

Haack, M., and C. Yocom. "State Policies and Nurses with Substance Use Disorders." *Journal of Nursing Scholarship* 34, no. 1 (2002): 89–94.

Hansen, M., B. Ganley, and C. Carlucci. "Journeys from Addiction to Recovery." *Research and Theory for Nursing Practice* 22 (2008): 256–72.

Hart, P. D. "Faces and Voices of Recovery Public Survey." Washington, DC: Peter D. Hart Research Associates, 2004.

Hedden, S. L. "Behavioral Health Trends in the United States: Results from the 2014 National Survey on Drug Use and Health." (2015). http://www.samhsa.gov/data/sites/default/files/NSDUH-FRR1-2014/NSDUH-FRR1-2014.pdf

Heise, B. "The Historical Context of Addiction in the Nursing Profession: 1850–1982." *Journal of Addictions Nurse* 14, no. 3 (2003): 117–24.

Horton-Deutsch, S., A. McNelis, and P. O'Haver Day. "Enhancing Mutual Accountability to Promote Quality, Safety, and Nurses' Recovery from Substance Use Disorders." *Archives of Psychiatric Nursing* 25 (2011): 445.

Kelly, J. F., R. Stout, W. Zywiak, and R. Schneider. "A 3–Year Study of Addiction Mutual-Help Group Participation Following Intensive Outpatient Treatment." *Alcoholism: Clinical and Experimental Research* 30 (2006): 1381–92.

Landry, M. J. Understanding Drugs of Abuse: The Processes of Addiction, Treatment and Recovery. Washington, DC: American Psychiatric Press, 1994.

Laudet, A. B. "What Does Recovery Mean to You? Lessons from the Recovery Experience for Research and Practice." *Journal of Substance Abuse Treatment* 33 (2007): 243–56.

Laudet, A. B., J. B. Becker, and W. L. White. "Don't Wanna Go through That Madness No More: Quality of Life Satisfaction as Predictor of Sustained Remission from Illicit Drug Misuse." *Substance Use & Misuse* 44 (2009): 227–52.

Margolis, R., A. Kilpatrick, and B. Mooney. "A Retrospective Look at Long-Term Adolescent Recovery: Clinicians Talk to Researchers." *Journal of Psychoactive Drugs* 32, no. 1 (2000): 117–25.

Masters, C., and D. S. Carlson. "The Process of Reconnecting: Recovery from the Perspective of Addicted Women." *Journal of Addictions Nursing* 17 (2006): 205–10.

McLellan, A. T., J. R. McKay, R. Forman, J. Cacciola, and J. Kemp. "Reconsidering the Evaluation of Addiction Treatment: From Retrospective Follow-up to Concurrent Recovery Monitoring." *Addiction* 100 (2005): 447–58.

McLellan, A. T., G. S. Skipper, M. Campbell, and R. L. DuPont. "Five Year Outcomes in a Cohort Study of Physicians Treated for Substance Use Disorders in the United States." *British Medical Journal* 337 (2008): a2038.

Merlo, L. J., and M. S. Gold. "Addiction Research and Treatment: The State of the Art in 2008." *Psychiatric Times* 25, no. 7 (2008): 52–57.

Millar, G., and L. Stermac. "Substance Abuse and Childhood Maltreatment." *The American Journal on Addictions* 22, no. 6 (2000): 605–12.

Monroe, T. B., and H. Kenaga. "Don't Ask Don't Tell: Substance Abuse and Addiction among Nurses." *Journal of Clinical Nursing* 20 (2010): 504–09.

National Council of State Boards of Nursing (NCSBN). "Substance Use Disorder in Nursing, a Resource Manual and Guidelines for Alternative and Disciplinary Monitoring Programs." (2011): 280.https://www.ncsbn.org/SUDN_11.pdf.

Payne, L. G. "Self-Acceptance and Its Role in Women's Recovery from Addiction." *Journal of Addictions Nursing* 21 (2010): 207–14.

Quinlan, D. "Impaired Nursing Practice: A National Perspective on Peer Assistance in the U.S." *Journal of Addictions Nursing* 14, no. 149–155 (2003).

Rassool, G. H., and S. Rawaf. "Predictors of Educational Outcomes of Undergraduate Nursing Students in Alcohol and Drug Education." *Nurse Education Today* 28 (2008): 691–701.

Srivastava, S., and M. S. Bhatia. "Quality of Life as an Outcome Measure in the Treatment of Alcohol Dependence." *Industrial Psychiatry Journal* 22, no. 1 (2013): 41–46.

Sullivan, E., and P. Decker. *Effective Leadership and Management in Nursing.* Upper Saddle River, NJ: Prentice Hall, 2001.

West, M. M. "Early Risk Indicators of Substance Abuse among Nurses." *Journal of Nursing Scholarship* 34, no. 2 (2002): 187–93.

Yocom, C., and M. Haack. Interim Report: A Comparison of Two Regulatory Approaches to the Management of the Chemically Dependent Nurse. Chicago, IL: National Council of State Boards of Nursing, 1996.

Young, L. J. "Education for Worksite Monitors of Impaired Nurses." *Nurse Administration Quarterly* 32, no. 4 (2008): 331–37.

IV

A QUALITATIVE STUDY: THE MEAN, METHOD, AND METHODOLOGY

Chapter Nine

Narrative Inquiry

The research methodology described as narrative inquiry is used in this study. Narrative inquiry is qualitative research that is used to explore the phenomenon of substance use and abuse through the stories shared by nurses who have personally dealt with these issues. This research study sought to answer three questions:

1. What stories do nurses tell about their personal experiences with substance use and abuse during various stages of their career?
2. What stories do nurses, who have successfully dealt with substance use disorders, tell about their recovery?
3. How do nurses describe the systems of support within the healthcare setting that helped them address their substance use disorder?

The following briefly describes the research design and rationale, the population and site targeted, the research methods used along with ethical considerations.

This qualitative research was designed to determine how the nurse participants view substance use and abuse and recovery and to obtain greater understanding of the phenomenon of addiction in their lives. Qualitative research is important as it attempts to understand different types of phenomena based on the significance and understandings people convey.[1] Narrative inquiry helps enlighten others to see and understand the human experience and involves interest, zeal, and empathy for its participants.[2] Narrative stories emerge from specific situations or places with the writer providing understanding and analysis of the stories told.[3] The sharing of personal narratives may encourage others to act. This is demonstrated by the ways stories circulate when social movements are forming; when individuals speak out, narratives invite others to mobilize and change.[4]

POPULATION AND RECRUITMENT

Seven nurses participated in this study. They were all nurses who have been living successfully in recovery for at least two years and nurses who also are participating or have previously participated in the California Board of Registered Nursing (BRN) Nurse Support Groups (NSGs). The nurses in these groups are in recovery and are usually monitored by the California BRN's Intervention or discipline programs. According to the California Nursing Practice Act,[5] for an individual involved with substance use to be allowed to participate in the Intervention Program, or be placed on probation, the individual must first be a registered nurse (RN); self-identify as having a substance use disorder; and be willing to comply with terms and conditions of the programs, which include abstaining from the misuse of drugs and or alcohol.

In 2014, in the State of California there were approximately 425 nurses in the Intervention Program and over 800 nurses on probation for substance abuse.[6] Over 2,000 nurses have successfully completed the California Intervention Program since it began in 1985, with much more successfully completing probation.[7] Although only a small representation of the over 400,000 registered nurses in California, the two programs offer a reliable source of nurses engaged in activities relating to substance use, abuse, and recovery.

The nurses participating in the study lived in California. Participants were required to: (a) be registered nurses, (b) have a minimum of two years' sobriety/recovery from substance abuse, (c) be participating or have previously participated in one of the California NSGs, and (d) be willing to voluntarily participate in three interviews. The nurses who volunteered to participate met the necessary qualifications and were chosen on a first come, first qualified basis.

Nurses were recruited from different NSGs in California. NSGs are group meetings facilitated by a volunteer RN who has expertise and understanding in the area of substance use disorders and who has been approved by the BRN. This individual has been designated as a volunteer to provide support regarding issues related to the process of recovery and re-entry into the workplace.[8] The NSGs were chosen because they are a reliable source of nurses engaged in recovery activities. All nurses who have come to the attention of the BRN for substance abuse, voluntarily or because of being disciplined, are required to attend a NSG. These NSGs have approximately 10 to 20 nurses attending each group and are independent support systems for the nurses. The nurses are required to attend a NSG once a week.[9]

The Deputy Chief of the BRN's Intervention and probation program was contacted and informed of the request to obtain volunteer participants from individual NSGs in California. The researcher provided her with a copy of the research invitation that outlined the information being sought and assured the participants' confidentiality. Once information regarding the request was provided, the researcher contacted the NSG facilitators and distributed approximately 178 letter/flyers describing the research to each facilitator for their distribution to the nurses in their group.[10] Facilitators were asked to pass out flyers to active participants within their perspective NSGs. The flyers described the planned research, requested volunteers, and contained the contact information of the researcher. It also requested that those receiving the flyer share with other nurses they may know who met the criteria.

NOTES

1. N. K. Denzin and Y. S. Lincoln, eds., Handbook of Qualitative Research 4ed. (Thousand Oaks, CA: Sage Publications, 2011).

2. D. J. Clandinin, Handbook of Narrative Inquiry: Mapping a Methodology (Thousand Oaks, CA: Sage Publications, Inc., 2007); B. Johnson and L. Christensen, Educational Research: Quantitative, Qualitative, and Mixed Methods, 5 ed. (Thousand Oaks, CA: Sage Publications, 2014).

3. J. W. Creswell, Educational Research: Planning, Conducting, and Evaluating Quantitative and Qualitative Research, 4 ed. (Upper Saddle River, NJ: Pearson, 2012).

4. C. K. Riessman, "Narrative Methods for the Human Sciences [Kindle]," Sage Publications.

5. California Board of Registered Nursing (BRN), Nursing Practice Act with Regulations and Related Statutes, (2016a), http://www.rn.ca.gov/regulations/npa.shtml.

6. Sunset Review Report, (2014), http://www.rn.ca.gov/pdfs/forms/sunset2014.pdf

7. California Board of Registered Nursing Board Meeting, Diversion/ Discipline Committee Meeting Agenda Item Summary, (2015), http://www.rn.ca.gov/pdfs/meetings/brd/brd_nov15_item9.pdf.

8. Ibid.

9. What Is the Intervention Program?, (2016b), http://www.rn.ca.gov/regulations/npa.shtml.

10. C. A. Stanford, "The Wake-up Call to Recovery: Drug Addiction and It's Effect on Registered Nurses: A Narrative Study" (Doctoral dissertation, Drexel University, 2017).

BIBLIOGRAPHY

California Board of Registered Nursing (BRN). *California Board of Registered Nursing Board Meeting, Diversion/ Discipline Committee Meeting Agenda Item Summary.* 2015. http://www.rn.ca.gov/pdfs/meetings/brd/brd_nov15_item9.pdf.

———. *Nursing Practice Act with Regulations and Related Statutes.* 2016a. http://www.rn.ca.gov/regulations/npa.shtml.

———. *Sunset Review Report.* 2014. http://www.rn.ca.gov/pdfs/forms/sunset2014.pdf

———. *What Is the Intervention Program?*, 2016b. http://www.rn.ca.gov/regulations/npa.shtml.

Clandinin, D. J. *Handbook of Narrative Inquiry: Mapping a Methodology.* Thousand Oaks, CA: Sage Publications, Inc., 2007. doi:10.4135/9781452226552.

Creswell, J. W. *Educational Research: Planning, Conducting, and Evaluating Quantitative and Qualitative Research.* 4 ed. Upper Saddle River, NJ: Pearson, 2012.

Denzin, N. K., and Y. S. Lincoln, eds. *Handbook of Qualitative Research* 4ed. Thousand Oaks, CA: Sage Publications, 2011.

Johnson, B., and L. Christensen. *Educational Research: Quantitative, Qualitative, and Mixed Methods.* 5 ed. Thousand Oaks, CA: Sage Publications, 2014.

Riessman, C. K. "Narrative Methods for the Human Sciences [Kindle]." Sage Publications.

Stanford, C. A. "The Wake-up Call to Recovery: Drug Addiction and It's Effect on Registered Nurses: A Narrative Study" Doctoral dissertation, Drexel University, 2017.

Chapter Ten

Data Collection

This research study made use of several data collection methods, including multiple interviews with each participant, participant journals, researcher observations, artifact (document) review, and a researcher's journal. In addition to interviews and journals, document review is a primary source of qualitative data.[1] It is a valuable resource for adding definitions, explanations, and insights and supplements participant interviews. Substance use, abuse, and recovery are abstract constructs; therefore, it is important that specific documents be used to clearly explain their meaning and definition. It is important there be construct validity, which required the researcher to clearly describe how substance use, abuse, and recovery had previously been represented or measured particularly in relation to the participants. Narrative scholars generally agree that narrative is not simply an honest account of events or circumstances, but it is instead an expression told from an individual's particular point of view. When there is correspondence between self-reports and archival evidence validity is strengthened.[2]

ARTIFACTS

Written records and historical documents were collected and reviewed regarding the BRN's Intervention and probation programs. This information detailed how the programs operate and how nurses with substance use disorders are identified and monitored. Additionally, individual artifacts from the participants such as memos and letters along with official correspondence were requested at the first interview to be brought to the second interview.[3] All identifying information in any documents provided was redacted. Documents and artifacts were obtained from the website and BRN headquarters.

The researcher obtained discipline records on those participants disciplined by BRN. They are considered public and were readily available.[4]

Detailed information and descriptions of the nurses, the BRN Intervention and probation programs, and other support systems as seen through the experiences of the nurse participants was outlined, analyzed and coded.[5] The data were consolidated, and results were interrelated and intertwined to develop themes or categories of ideas where appropriate. Narrative study, however, relies on extended accounts that are preserved and treated analytically as units. These accounts cannot always be divided into separate categories or themes.[6] As the researcher, I had to understand and enter the world of the nurse participants. The nurse participants' viewpoint was explored in order to understand and draw themes, results, and conclusions in relation to all the components of the research.[7]

The narrative stories provide the opportunity for those who have been voiceless to speak. Therefore, where necessary, some narratives were reported separately and comprehensively. Excerpts from actual statements of the participants were used. Allowing individuals to speak in their own voice provides genuine discoveries, offers different perspectives, and delivers a complex picture about the phenomenon of substance use and abuse.[8]

ETHICAL CONSIDERATIONS

During this study, there were ethical considerations built into the research design. As part of the protection that occurred for the participants, I went through the Drexel Institutional Review Board (IRB) process. This process complies with the legal aspects and policies related to ethical standards and integrity established by the National Institute of Health. It is a process designed to protect the welfare of human subjects in research. As part of the process, prior to partaking in the research study, the participants were provided a consent form to obtain verbal consent and initials.

The study was designed to assure that there was no potential for harm. To maintain participants' anonymity, pseudonyms were used throughout the project. It is important the participants have the ability to preserve their privacy and throughout the study, participants were only identified by their pseudonym. Additionally, extra care was taken to assure the confidentiality of the participants in accord with policies established through the Drexel IRB process. To assure that there was complete confidentiality, the planned location to interview the participants was at a private location of their choice. Recordings and transcriptions were maintained on drives without Internet access.

NOTES

1. L. D. Bloomberg and M. Volpe, Completing Your Qualitative Dissertation: A Roadmap from Beginning to End, 3 ed. (Los Angeles: Sage Publications, 2016).

2. C. K. Riessman, "Narrative Methods for the Human Sciences [Kindle]," Sage Publications.

3. J. W. Creswell, Educational Research: Planning, Conducting, and Evaluating Quantitative and Qualitative Research, 4 ed. (Upper Saddle River, NJ: Pearson, 2012).

4. J. E. Porter and T. R. Mackay, "Collateral Damage to Encumbered Nursing Licenses," Journal of Nursing Law 15, no. 2 (2012).

5. C. A. Stanford, "The Wake-up Call to Recovery: Drug Addiction and It's Effect on Registered Nurses: A Narrative Study " (Doctoral dissertation, Drexel University, 2017).

6. Riessman, "Narrative Methods for the Human Sciences [Kindle]."

7. B. Johnson and L. Christensen, Educational Research: Quantitative, Qualitative, and Mixed Methods, 5 ed. (Thousand Oaks, CA: Sage Publications, 2014).

8. Creswell, Educational Research: Planning, Conducting, and Evaluating Quantitative and Qualitative Research; Riessman, "Narrative Methods for the Human Sciences [Kindle]"

BIBLIOGRAPHY

Bloomberg, L. D., and M. Volpe. *Completing Your Qualitative Dissertation: A Roadmap from Beginning to End.* 3 ed. Los Angeles: Sage Publications, 2016.

Creswell, J. W. *Educational Research: Planning, Conducting, and Evaluating Quantitative and Qualitative Research.* 4 ed. Upper Saddle River, NJ: Pearson, 2012.

Johnson, B., and L. Christensen. *Educational Research: Quantitative, Qualitative, and Mixed Methods.* 5 ed. Thousand Oaks, CA: Sage Publications, 2014.

Porter, J. E., and T. R. Mackay. "Collateral Damage to Encumbered Nursing Licenses." *Journal of Nursing Law* 15, no. 2 (2012): 45–50.

Riessman, C. K. "Narrative Methods for the Human Sciences [Kindle]." Sage Publications.

Stanford, C. A. "The Wake-up Call to Recovery: Drug Addiction and It's Effect on Registered Nurses: A Narrative Study" Doctoral dissertation, Drexel University, 2017.

V

THE VOICES: THE DYNAMICS AND SUFFERINGS OF ADDICTION

"I had to change in order to be healthy . . . I grew up in an alcoholic family.
The family dynamics affected who I was and how I interacted with the world."

—Mimosa

Chapter Eleven

The Nurses

This chapter introduces the seven participants followed by chapters representing the findings that emerged from the analysis of the participant stories and a parallel analysis of artifacts and observational notes. These findings are supported with rich, descriptive excerpts in the participants' voices. The data presented inform the research results, which are interpreted considering prior research.

The seven participants in this narrative study were all registered nurses in California. They spanned several age generations. Based on their years of nursing service and their indicated years in recovery, these individuals practiced nursing while untreated for alcohol and or drug use for an average of 19 years (Range = 6-27 years). Six of the participants were female and one participant was male, and all participants were Caucasian. Two completed their initial nursing education while residing in another country.

Three of the participants have been formally disciplined by the State of California as a result of their alcohol and or drug use. One had her registered nursing (RN) license revoked for approximately two years. Two participants had escaped discipline and voluntarily joined a nurse support group affiliated with the Intervention (Diversion) Program. Several of the participants had been enrolled in the Intervention Program.

Table 11:1 provides information on the participants: (a) pseudonym, (b) age, (c) employment during alcohol/drug use, (d) current nursing employment status, and (e) years in recovery. Pseudonyms based on names of flowers were selected by each participant.

Heather retired after 54 years in nursing. She has been in recovery for 32 years, and she described recovery as a "gift" not provided to nurses due to the professional stigma that exists against nurses with substance use disorders. "I believe the healthcare industry still has a stigma with nurses who have a

Table 11.1.   Table 11.1. Participant Overview

Pseudonym	Age	Years in Nursing	Employment During Use	Current Employment	Years in Recovery
Heather	70	54	Hospital	Retired	32
Jasmine Jade	54	23	Catheter. Lab, Diagnostics	Cardio Vascular	7
Mimosa	77	56	Surgery Department	Retired	47
Morning Glory	39	12	Emergency & Oncology	Case Management	6
Purple Lilly	38	14	Labor & Delivery	Case Management	2
Napeta	60	43	Emergency Psych. Med. Surg. HIV	Heart Surgical Center	16
Rose	41	18	Surgery Center	Case Management	6

problem with alcohol or drugs. There's a stigma and because of that you know the pathways aren't open. They aren't open for identifying the nurses, treating the nurses, backing up the nurses. It's just not available." (Heather)

Jasmine Jade has worked as a registered nurse for 23 years and has been in recovery for the recent seven years. She currently works as a traveling nurse. She says she is "living proof" that recovery and rehabilitation do happen. However, she stated that because of the stigma of addiction, employers will not hire her.

> Nurses with a history of alcoholism and addiction don't get to work. It all has to be a secret . . . Once the Board of Nursing put me on probation, no hospitals ever hired me full time again. Sometimes brutal honesty doesn't land you a job, because they don't believe that nurses can rehabilitate. They believe that nurses, once they cope with alcohol or drugs, or whatever it is they do, that they are unable [to perform]. That's not true, I am living proof that it can happen . . . How do we change the stigma? . . . why would you do that to your own people? Because . . . we're not revenue. We are cost . . . then they don't want you. That's why they're kicking out nurses. (Jasmine Jade)

Mimosa, the oldest participant, was a registered nurse for 56 years, and had been in recovery for 47 years. She was never reported to the state board for her drug use by her employer; rather, she voluntarily went to the first nurse support groups. She indicated that recovery "enhanced" her personal life, "in recovery, I found that my whole world opened up. Not only for me, but to me."

Morning Glory at 39 was one of the younger nurses participating. She had been a registered nurse for 12 years and in recovery for six years. She described managers within the healthcare community as being ruthless and uninformed. She was told by one that she "would never work . . . again." "They basically booted me out the door and said 'you're bad get out! We're done with you!' I felt discarded." She described having "no professional support" and had to redefine her value while in the recovery process. "I would walk into AA meetings and I would say 'I'm . . . I'm a nurse.' And that's all I knew how to be, and they would say 'I don't f*** care what you are. You're an alcoholic.' And I had to learn that I had value in other places." (Morning Glory). Today Morning Glory is successfully employed and working in case management.

Napeta had been a registered nurse for 43 years and had 16 years of recovery. Working as a bedside nurse in several areas, Napeta expressed confidence in recovery.

> I'm extremely involved because after all the clean time and the sobriety I have, I have no problem outing myself because I'm the safest nurse . . . I'm a nurse in recovery. That is the big difference. I am a recovered nurse. I'm not using anything so that is, if you cultivate that attitude for yourself, that makes you also develop that self-love again that you don't be ashamed. (Napeta)

Purple Lilly, 38, had been a registered nurse for 14 years, and had two and a half years of recovery. Working in case management without access to narcotics, Purple Lilly spoke about the gift of recovery.

> I mean, I'm so grateful that I do feel like my nursing career and the path that I chose, helped me get here in a way that was very unique, and I would have ended up here anyways, no matter what I chose to do for a living . . . But I feel like I've been sort of given this gift, that it sort of infiltrates every area of my life. And I, I, I don't know how I lived so long without this life; but, I know people who get sober at 60. (Purple Lilly)

Rose has been a registered nurse for 18 years and has been in recovery for six years. She is working as a case manager doing discharge planning, care utilization, and patient review. In describing her job, she noted, "I really enjoy it because it doesn't involve the labor-intensive work of the bedside staff nurse. I also get to work with the patient, work with the team, work in a hospital, which I've always really enjoyed." She says the promises of recovery are real.

> I did what . . . [they] said. You get a sponsor. You go to meetings. You do the steps. You're honest, open. You're willing. Step one, two, three. Just do it. Of

course, the addict mind was talking saying, "just do it for two years and then you can tell them this didn't work for me, thank you, goodbye." But it happened. I got sober for real. . . when I got into recovery, the hole was filled up with God. Yes, I feel full, but it's a spiritual feeling. (Rose)

Six of the seven participants met with the researcher multiple times and participated in three separate interviews; the seventh participant participated in two interviews (see Stanford, 2017 for additional information regarding interviewing, coding, and analysis processes).

Five themes emerged from the voices and experiences of the participants: (a) family dynamics and patterns; (b) substance use disorders in nurse education and within the nurse profession; (c) illusions and secrets of the nurse professional; (d) confrontational "crisis" and the "wake-up call;" and (e) recovery, spiritual awakenings and recovery communities.

Chapter Twelve

Family Dynamics and Patterns

Mimosa clearly articulated the issues facing nurses with a family history of addiction stating, "I had to change in order to be healthy. I grew up in an alcoholic family. The family dynamics affected who I was and how I interacted with the world."

FAMILY HISTORY OF DRUG AND ALCOHOL ABUSE

All the participants referenced some type of family dynamic and substance abuse among family members. They described the role substance use played in their addiction and reliance on substances.

> At the time even when I was in school my brother was actively active in his addiction . . . my dad died while I was in school from his addiction . . . I grew up in a family that was just destroyed by addiction, my dad's side of the family. There's just a ton of people who died. I had a cousin who was a physician in the emergency department . . . died of an opiate overdose. And no one knew what he was doing until he died . . . We can trace back, I mean my grandfather to my uncles, my dad . . . And then my brother, when he was 13, he ran away and started living on the streets . . . was involved in cocaine and selling meth . . . it was almost like from day one. He was looking for something. That was the solution . . . he was smoking weed and getting drunk at 11. (Morning Glory)

Mimosa also states, "My father's alcohol affected my life gravely, when I was a child. He would become rageful, he would hit on us . . . we don't talk about it. We still don't. I've tried to, but they don't want to acknowledge it."

Rose disclosed, "My dad drank a lot . . . He was an alcoholic for sure . . . My brother, he started smoking weed at 13 and he's still on that path. He

binge drinks, does cocaine, but he's maintaining his job and relationship."
Heather shared, "My family dies. I just buried a sister in December . . .
committed suicide, alcoholic. I'm from a very long line of alcoholics . . . I am
the only one in my family that has recovery. I have a brother who died of
alcoholism at 52."

Experiences with drug experimentations, overdoses, and deaths due to
substance abuse, as well as physical and emotional abuse during childhood
provided a foundation for their entry into alcohol and drug use. Heather
framed this as, "if you're going to be an alcoholic, you're going to be an
alcoholic. . . I do believe that it is in the genes. I do believe it is part of nature
and nurture, growing up in an alcoholic environment."

EARLY DRUG AND
ALCOHOL USE DURING CHILDHOOD YEARS

Several participants described their introduction to alcohol and drug use at
early ages (11, 16, or 17). Morning Glory, Rose, and Mimosa opened up
about their childhood experiences.

> My dad had alcohol everywhere . . . my dad wouldn't know if a little was
> missing. And we were always around it, he had a lot of friends that would
> come over and bring alcohol or whatever . . . I remember doing things to get
> alcohol . . . it wasn't that hard . . . I don't remember the first time I drank. I
> know I tried beer. Like really young. Like it was just around, it's just what
> everybody was doing, so. But I remember being 11 and being on the elemen-
> tary school campus on the weekends and smoking weed . . . Yeah, out of like a
> Coke can, we would flatten the coke can and poke holes in it and that was our
> "little Bong," well not Bong, but little pipe. And I mean, I don't even know
> how I got it. It was just all the kids in the neighborhood or whatever . . . my
> dad would have weed around. It was just there. It was just life. It seemed like it
> was just normal for me. (Morning Glory)

> I started at 16 . . . My friend and I went out to the shed and looked at all the
> alcohol, and I got the highest volume which was Brandy . . . a fifth, and I just
> strawed it all down. I blacked out . . . I remember feeling it and I loved it. It
> was so much fun . . . I did throw up and I had a headache, but I couldn't wait to
> do it again . . . But I waited till the weekend . . . I was binging . . . Then, started
> taking drugs because the rave culture was huge in . . . in the '90s. We'd take
> ecstasy and acid . . . Started taking E [Ecstasy] tablets and acid at age 17 as
> well as drinking . . . It was all on the weekends. (Rose)

> Drinking was first. It probably happened at the same time that most people—I
> was in nursing school, I was a basketball player, and one of my peer's boy-
> friends said, "Have you ever been drunk?" And I said, "No." He said, "Well,
> you should find out what it's like." And so, I proceeded to do that, before a

basketball practice, and oh God. How old was I? I was 17 when I went into nursing school. (Mimosa)

Whatever their age, as Napeta described, at some point, use became abuse:

> In the neighborhood bar, I learned from other people who were, well you can't just get drunk and be an idiot. You have to contain yourself . . . And then in one moment, we cross this invisible line and all of a sudden, the switch is pulled. (Napeta)

Most of the participants revealed how family influences and dynamics around substance use and abuse had a lasting effect on their lives and the way they viewed drug and alcohol use.

> I did grow up in a pretty chaotic home in my life . . . so my relationships with my parents had always been quite strained, but definitely when I am drinking and using I will take that to a whole new level of disrespect and cut people out of my life just, just running, just constantly running to be alone with my disease. I wasn't able to have friends—authentic friendships, nobody really knew me. (Purple Lilly)

All seven participants grew up around family members who were affected in some manner by drugs or alcohol. They were introduced to drugs and alcohol in their childhood and began experimenting with alcohol or drugs in their teens and appeared to cope with life and its stresses by escaping through substance use.

Chapter Thirteen

Substance Use Disorders in Nursing Education and Within the Nursing Profession

DRUG AND ALCOHOL USE
IN NURSING SCHOOL AND EARLY CAREER

Jasmine Jade explained, "It started off innocently. Partying after a hard day's work, and during college, of course, we all experimented . . . it was the norm." Mimosa shared, "I was in nursing school . . . My abuse started there, because there was stuff on the shelf that was just free. I found some of the stuff made me feel good." Rose similarly expressed, "The brain will tell you that it is normal, because you are in this college culture. Everyone is doing it." She described how while she was in nursing school she, "stole sleeping pills from the medicine cart to sleep."

Purple Lilly described how her early experimentation with drugs came without fear:

> I was a nurse at the time, but it was just in my social life. It was . . . Ecstasy and party drugs. What it was, is that I knew that drugs changed the way I felt, and I also knew out the gates that I wasn't normal around there use, and I wasn't sure what the reason, what the impacts of this would be; but, if it was anything like what I experienced, I was all in. I was willing to figure it out. There wasn't a fear. I think most people don't do drugs because they are afraid of what it's going to do to them. That wasn't a fear for me . . . But, I also think experimenting with the drugs with people I trusted, lessened my inhibitions and my concerns about it. And made it really no big deal . . . If I had not done street drugs, I don't think I even would have questioned wanting. I don't even

know if I would have connected that that would have been something I would
have been into. (Purple Lilly)

Rose revealed that the year after she graduated, [I] "stole my first tramadol tablet." Three years later, she moved to a major city and "for four years
drank a lot, took drugs on weekends mostly, E [ecstasy] and cocaine." Morning Glory revealed, "I got a DUI while I was in college." She further described how friends who were nurses introduced her to stealing drugs:

> My first experience was one of my friends who worked at a different hospital
> and was a nurse; she had been a nurse for a lot longer time than me. I go over
> to her house one night and we're going to go out partying, whatever you want
> to call it. And both her and her husband were nurses. And I said, "Oh I have a
> headache. I don't know maybe I shouldn't go out tonight." And she brought
> me into her room and she opened up a drawer in her bedroom and she said,
> "Here look. You know take something for your headache. Let's go out." And
> she had Vicodin and Dilaudid and everything and I was like, "Oh where did
> you get this?" And she said, "Well I just take from work when I can, but you
> know." That nurse that showed me, that opened that drawer that day in her
> apartment in . . . I'd been working as a nurse about probably a year and a half
> or something. Yeah. And so and it never occurred to me until she opened that
> door and then oh man... she opened that world to me. . . . So, you know that
> was my education. Like, I was like you can just take home the extras . . .
>
> She doesn't have a license today. She got caught. She went and started
> working at another hospital, she got caught there. She started working at
> another hospital and by the time they finally caught up with her and took her
> license, she worked at five hospitals in two years. . . . I don't know about her
> husband, but he was stealing drugs too. And so, I don't know if he ever got
> caught, but I know that she lost her license and never tried to get it back. And I
> needed to like just to separate from her because she was very sick, so I still
> wonder about her. As for as I know, she didn't want to go into recovery. She
> didn't have a 'problem' . . . Sometimes you wonder, why did I run into that
> person? But . . . it was just progressive . . . (Morning Glory)

LACK OF KNOWLEDGE AND EDUCATION ABOUT ADDICTION

All seven participants indicated they had received little education about substance abuse or risk factors related to drugs or alcohol in nursing school.
Morning Glory, who had recently completed her graduate degree in nursing,
described herself as . . . "shocked at how little education I received, . . . we
barely scratched the surface of what addiction was. I have two uncles that
died young. I mean, so I knew that alcoholism and addiction existed; but, I
certainly didn't gain any insight in school . . . which is crazy!" (Morning
Glory)

Heather, educated in the 1950s, similarly shared:

Do you know I didn't get any education about addiction when I was in nursing school and I was trained by the Harvard doctors and they did not get any special training in alcoholism. So, throughout my career there was no special education about training me about addiction. There just wasn't. My original nursing education was what was called a diploma program and I trained for three years at a city hospital in . . . and because it was a city hospital we had lots of alcoholics as patients and we had lots of their family members as patients. Do you know it was the late 50's 1958, I went into training? While alcoholism had been declared a disease, it certainly hadn't filtered down to the healthcare of alcoholics. Basically, they were still treated pretty badly.

I remember one protocol in . . . and I remember very clearly in those days, if you were admitted and you were stinking drunk we would wait for you to go into the DT's (detox) before we treated you. That was the protocol and people die in the DT's. It is constant seizure, that's what the DT's are it is constant seizing and then we would give them this drug called Paraldehyde. I never forget it because it smelled so bad. But there was no education— we as nursing students had no education. . . . Paraldehyde—This was the drug of choice for treating alcoholics. So, once we got them out of the DTs we would give them Librium and that was about it. But most of all what was important was that there was no calling this a disease. This was not a disease. This was a, this was a disgrace. This was a bad, bad person that was drinking too much. That sentiment was held by the doctors and again I am talking about Harvard University Medical School. (Heather)

Mimosa exclaimed, "We didn't learn anything about the disease or people using drugs in school, and I don't know that I saw it in the workplace, although I do remember being around people that probably had a problem." Napeta shared, "In nursing school, there was like little about addictionology, addiction in nursing. And most of it I learned by working in emergency and lock down psych." Rose reflecting on her more recent training summed it up, "I don't remember anything about addiction at all. I remember nothing about alcoholism addiction."

Jasmine Jade further states:

We went through the education training; I actually did a clinical in Psych where we actually experienced the lock-down. But, it was more geared towards people that had eating disorders and had a history of cocaine abuse, that kind of thing - never alcohol, though. Alcohol was probably involved, but these were really lock-down patients. That was my experience in nursing school. I understood that there was a disease process when it came to that. But, I never really connected the two-- the grief pattern. I missed that point, but I know that they went over it. The thing about it is maybe in more detail it would've stuck because I was older. I was already 29 when I started. (Jasmine Jade)

Rose expresses her concern for nursing students while sharing her experience:

If you feel like you have a problem, if you can't stop after a couple of drinks, there is something going on. You don't want to wait until the consequences start happening, because the Board of Nursing is not as tolerant now, I don't think. I have seen three people get their nursing licenses revoked. My advice would be to—I guess in school if you have some counselor available to you, talk to them about your problems and they could give you resources. If you can't stop drinking and it's so toxic in your body the level until your brain shuts down, you have a problem. That's not normal. The brain will tell you that it is normal, because you are in this college culture. Everyone is doing it. If you wait until the consequences happens, DUI, relationships, you could injure yourself, you could injure somebody else, that's up to you, unfortunately.

The alcoholic mind is very alive. It talks to you, it schemes. That's why students need to talk to somebody if they feel like they have a problem. Because you have not come through the recovery process, so you don't know the difference between really, honestly, what is normal and what is not normal. The alcoholic mind is not normal. It lies and manipulates. It only became overpowered from my experience through doing the 12 steps the right way the second time, the first time I didn't do them the right way. (Rose)

Mimosa suggested that professional nursing education regarding substance abuse is regressing, and any gains that had been made in the past regarding rehabilitation and recovery for nurses were being lost. "Nurses . . . are reinventing the wheel . . . because they have to educate their administrators, their nursing directors, HR people, the fact that it's a disease, and nurses respond well to treatment, and that they don't need to be thrown away, because that's what I've seen." (Mimosa)

Heather emphatically declared:

The basic foundation of our industry is still that being an addict is a shameful entity . . . If the core belief is this is a disease that effects people, then that's the core foundation and that really determines what will and will not happen so there is very little education about it. There are very little information out there about what resources are available. There is a lot of blocking of the resources for nurses. It's very distressing, it's very distressing, because nurses are almost seen as a throw away commodity! (Heather)

Jasmine Jade further noted, "You don't get an opportunity to learn. You're just terrified; it's like a bully system."

I was getting beat up at home and trying to come to work and hiding it and I finally went to my boss and that's when I said, "There's a problem. I'm having problems at home I may need your help." Instead of looking at me like help, they were like, 'No, you're just drinking too much," Then I ended up saying "I don't give a damn anymore!" (Jasmine Jade)

SELF-MEDICATION, WORK STRESS, AND ACCESS

According to Jasmine Jade, "Just being a nurse is stressful . . . alcohol works in the beginning for all of us for stress relief. But then one day it turns against you. It causes, you to become more dependent on it to help deal, cope effectively."

Rose stated:

> If you drink to reach a level of comfort, then it's self-medicating and it's just a Band Aid. You have to address the issues such as anxiety, nervousness, depression, low self-esteem, et cetera. It's the optimal option for a long-term, well-adjusted development – alcohol, until it stops working. It stops working and then you're left with yourself! (Rose)

Mimosa elaborated about how she learned to cope with challenging situations:

> When under stress . . . what they learn in . . . families . . . you grab something to make you feel better and . . . where isn't their stress in nursing and access, you know. Maybe you're not going to drink a beer or a shot, but, ooh, this little drug over here may help me. But, I think that's how it happens. (Mimosa)

Mimosa further described how she was promoted to a head nurse early in her career with her addiction to prescription drugs flourishing:

> I would sporadically find something that looked good, so I'd try it, and I'm trying to remember the name of that first drug, it had a funny name. But then also I had a lot of problems with cramps, when I got my period, Dysmenorrhea, it's called, and I found this wonderful drug, called . . . Daprisol. It had speed in it . . . and then, run around like a crazy lady. I always felt like I was really accomplishing things when I was taking it . . . Ambar . . . I found this whole great big bottle so that lasted a while. Of course, I got to the . . . U . . . and became a head nurse very early in my career. I would just ask one of the doctors to write me a prescription for Daprisol or Edrisol. First, I'd say, "Give me a prescription for a big one, we'll keep it here for everybody." Most of it went to me . . . oh God - awful. Today, I think about -- terrible. It's sad that – But I didn't know I had a disease and even did not accept that for a long time. (Mimosa)

Jasmine Jade reported, "We become addicted to our work. I wasn't just addicted to alcohol; I was addicted to adrenaline. I was addicted to being under that kind of pressure and stress in the cath. lab. I was addicted to working out." Jasmine Jade further declared:

> All of us nurses, I don't care who you are if you have poor coping mechanisms, you bring your work home and you nurture it and then you go back into

it, so you never have relief of the stress. Never have relief of the stress and then soon it's like you're carrying the world on your shoulders. You're weighed down and that's when you start falling and skinning your knees and then instead of going around the pit you go into the pit. Because you're not light, you haven't shed that stress. (Jasmine Jade)

Napeta confided a story about the stresses occurring in his personal life and the impact it had on his job.

And then when the crisis hit which was my divorce, or a loss of . . . or being alone because addiction is a disease of loneliness. So, I felt after the divorce that I was lonely and then I was depressed. And so, for some reason I had a leftover Demerol in my pocket at the end of the shift, sometimes these things happen, and I normally would discard those into the appropriate places, that's the Pyxis. And for some reason I thought it was a good idea and took that home and took that. That was the only time I did that at home, and then it escalated into where I would when I'd be off work, I would not use and had no problems not using, and would use exclusively at work, so, therefore, I'm a big understander of nurses, stress and excess.

So, once they're there, then depending on their personality—wherever that carries one. So, 10% of the now population is afflicted with the disease of this or with an ism. Because as we know there are different isms; shopping, working, controlling, I don't know, domestic violence; all kinds of stuff going on so an ism and so 10% have it or even more. In nursing it's higher because of again stress and access and of the thing the nurses heal themselves, which is of course total misconception of self-diagnosing. (Napeta)

ADDICTION COMPULSIONS, SOLITARY SUFFERING, AND SPIRITUAL MALADY

Purple Lilly explained the power drugs had over her:

I first started using opiates, which was my drug of choice, I was diverting from a surgery center that I was working at . . . behold I followed myself! Right! And . . . people will ask me "When did you decide to start using?" And I don't know. I remember going home one night with a syringe in my pocket that I was supposed to waste, and I didn't. And instead of like thinking oh I should probably bring this back tomorrow, I kept it in my closet for weeks. And then I used, and it was all over from there. I mean I'd done some drugs before, so I knew I wasn't normal around drugs. But immediately, I knew that I would be seeking that feeling. And from that day on, it was all I could do was to figure out how to get more. (Purple Lilly)

Rose described an escalating experience with substances and how her behavior became bizarre.

I moved up to the other hospital . . . and that's where it all went down. The very first time that I stole there was—I had a half a dose of morphine left in my pocket from a patient who decided that they didn't want all of it. They decided just half of it, and then I was hung-over . . . I was hung-over from alcohol. I had a banging headache. I remember thinking, "Oh, I should take the morphine because then my headache would go away." I injected it in my muscle and it worked and I was off to the races. Yes, so for one year I did it . . . morphine wasn't good enough, and Dilaudid then . . . because I worked in a liver unit and I would see how there is a lot of patients addicted to Dilaudid. They want it, they want it, they want it and you see them, they relax. So, I wanted to try that. Then that was the one that was highly addictive. I did it IV . . . it's crazy, yes, it's pretty wild. I did it in the hospital and then I started taking them home.

I remember when I first started at . . . they told me a nurse got fired for stealing drugs and I thought to myself, "Oh what a criminal." That's funny. First couple of days, that was the person I replaced, they told me. Because I had a dichotomy going on and I compartmentalized my life. I didn't see it as an issue that I took the Tramadol in the hospital in . . . and I didn't do it again, stealing, because I got it online. Then I went on there and, I hadn't had that morphine incident. I was innocent, I'm so pure, "Oh what a criminal that person is." (Rose)

Rose further depicted how her substance abuse progressed:

I did it, yes. I didn't even think about it . . . then I knew after the first (Dilaudid) it's a raging drive and force. It just opens some floodgate where you can't stop thinking about how you're going to get your next chance. I will go in early and look at the patients and the big stack of papers for all the patients. And I would go through and see who was on Dilaudid and I would grab them and say, "I will take this patient. I will take this patient," . . . nobody noticed. One person asked me, "Why was my hand so swollen," because I used to wear long sleeves and my hand was all swollen from missing veins. And then I said, "Oh I hit it." That was the only time somebody had noticed anything, I just said, "I hit it."

Then towards the end of that year, the Dilaudid kind of stopped working. Yes, and I took Demerol and I felt drunk, at work. I was handing off my patients to somebody, and she said, "Are you, all right?" I said, "I'm okay." I had some excuse, a headache or something. That really scared me, so I didn't take it at work--I took it maybe two or three times . . . I would take it when I got home, definitely. It's amazing and even sometimes on my days off I would say, "I want to go by the hospital really quick. I have to get something," and I would go in and take it and leave . . . I met one nurse one time and I said, "I'm working on another floor," I was just such a liar. Such a liar . . . You go into this robotic mode, it's very bizarre. You can't stop it. (Rose)

According to all the participants, addiction has a power that is ever-present. Disciplinary records obtained from State of California stated Rose was unable to stay sober and was terminated from the state's Intervention (Diversion) program for several relapses and testing positive for cocaine. She stated, "I was terminated from diversion for relapsing . . . Started drinking again regularly and injecting cocaine because alcohol didn't have a high enough high anymore."

Jasmine Jade reported, "When I got my first DUI I should've stopped then, but I didn't and then I got my second DUI—I should have stopped then and I just went through the probation and I chose not to drink and drive." Purple Lilly revealed how she experienced a personal health crisis and yet continued to steal and use drugs from work despite any fears and negative consequences:

> I had my first seizure and was taken off work for two weeks. I had been using a couple months by now like I developed a tolerance to some degree by then. I either passed out or had a seizure because I didn't pee on myself or anything. I know that I fell to the ground and I was there knocked out cold until my sister came and knocked on my door. So, two weeks go by I go back to work. . . I remember being up at my parents' house and . . . thinking about ways that I could stop. "How can I stop?" I so desperately wanted to stop, but, couldn't. And so, I went back to work, and everyone was like, "what happened?" and I would tell them. "I had a seizure. I was on seizure medication." Not one single person in my medical job thought to drug test me or say anything. That was July. So, from July to December I'm still off and running, diverting every day; faking the books, nobody's catching on. I'm just going about my business. No big deal.
>
> December 15th for some reason or actually I'd gotten in a fight with my mom the night before, and I went to work, and I had used the night before. And for the first time, and I'm not sure why, I decided to that day, I used at work in the bathroom and I had this thought of like "OK now this is getting to a whole new level." And it scared me. But then I went back to work . . . and was super excited that I had more drugs in my purse for when I was going to get home which I never got to use because I passed out at work. And fell to the floor and was taken by ambulance to the hospital next door with a big gash on my head. And they went through my purse to get my phone to call my mom and that's when they saw the Demerol in my purse. So that's when the gig was up. I mean, I think I even had a vial in my pocket. I'm not sure, but it was like they were clear on what was going on. And then my boss came to me and said, "I know what's going on," and I was like, "no." Like I totally tried to lie about it. (Purple Lilly)

Purple Lilly admitted how her addiction kept her from others and kept her alone and uncommitted.

> Drugs and alcohol and my eating disorder makes it almost impossible for me to be completely present in a relationship. And although . . . I can be so manipulative I can fake it for a while. But the truth is that the addiction always wins, always. Always! . . . when I'm in my disease I keep people at a distance so that I don't have to be committed to anything. So, I can always have a way

out and be with my drug of choice, whatever that may be at the time. (Purple Lilly)

Morning Glory described her personal suffering and the personal reaction to being caught diverting from work:

> They told me you know you need to call. Here's the number to call for Diversion and we're going to call them too so if you don't call them you'll be reported to the Board. So, I was like, "OK I'll call them," because you know, I know I'm not stupid . . . so. I called on my own. That night I, I got really, really, really wasted and was just alone and just miserable. You know, freaking out . . . But you know I got up and I called like my only friend really that I had left. And her and her boyfriend came and they, we broke my lease. They packed my apartment up in . . . Came back to . . .with her and she said you're calling Diversion today. You know we called, I called, and they did the intake like in the next day . . . And I remember sitting there at her house doing the intake on the phone and just, I mean I thought my life was over. You know, I just wanted to die. (Morning Glory)

Rose believed that substance abuse reflected a "spiritual malady," "When you're in it, alcoholics can be very immature, very childish. I believe it's a *spiritual malady*. It's a soul sickness from a very young age and the hole for me was filled up by cookies, alcohol, drugs. Then when I got into recovery the hole was filled up with God. Yes, I feel full, but it's a spiritual feeling."

Morning Glory was unsuccessful in the California Diversion (Intervention) program:

> I [after the program] got set up in some like depression bullshit thing . . . I did not have depression . . . It was not depression. It was all addiction, all of it. It was that *spiritual malady*. I mean and that's what everyone you talk to with addiction reaches the point where either they just want to die, or they don't care if they live anymore or they try to kill themselves. That's what happens. Like that's what we do. And people need to know that. But I had all these people telling me though in the hospital the psychiatrist in the psych hospital was like you know, we think you're bipolar and stuff. And I'm not bipolar. But, I also would say "No, I don't drink that much." And I would be going to the depression group and I'm not in Diversion anymore, so I would go in the depression group and then go home and drink and get wasted and then wake up hung over the next day go to group and be like, "oh I'm so depressed." Well, yeah, cause you're f*** hung over. (Morning Glory)

All the participants used drugs and or alcohol while in nursing school and early in their nursing careers. Whether attending nursing school in the 1950s or the early 2000s none of the participants remembered having curriculum in nursing school or early in their careers that addressed the nurses' susceptibility to drug abuse. The participants shared the power that substance use had over their lives despite consequences and their own desires to stop the use. They spoke about how their solitary efforts to overcome addiction were futile and realized there was an inner soul malady. They believed the problem was compounded by the stress of work and the access to substances.

Chapter Fourteen

Illusions and Secrets
of the Nurse Professional

DECEPTIONS AND UNREALISTIC
VIEWS OF THE ADDICTED NURSE

Several of the participants described how the moniker "nurse" provided an image of goodness that shielded their substance abuse issues. Morning Glory shared that, despite any of her criminal or addictive behavior, she was not held culpable for her actions because she looked a certain way and she was a nurse.

> I had to show up in court once a month for like 13 months and they dropped it . . . They looked at me and they said, "Oh sweetheart you're OK." You know they were like, "You're doing a great job girl, good job." Cause then I'm sitting there. I, I'm sitting around people who you know, and it just makes me sick. Yeah, because you know what, my brother he's a felon he's, he's been, he was in prison. And he, he has a whole different experience when people look at him. And he's got tattoos and he's got, and you know we're not different. Let me tell you, we're not different. (Morning Glory)

She further elaborated:

> It's not right you know, but yeah. But, I think too the fact that I was a nurse, because I've heard other nurses have that experience. And I tell you, I mean I think racism, sexism is prevalent in this country; however, I also think classism is a huge, huge problem, bigger than anything, bigger than anything else . . . I got it together and I looked OK . . . And I had that nursing degree and for whatever reason I was able to do that. And that got me through the criminal part. You know what I mean, like it really did and so, I think that's weird. I mean there's, I know people. I know a dentist who did the same thing. I know

a couple of doctors who did the same thing. I know another nurse practitioner who did the same thing. We all had that same experience where we're smart, we're professional; we know how to hold ourselves. We look good on paper, so we don't need no help. We're not like "those other people," yeah, and it sucks. It's not, it's not OK. We need to all – we're all the same. (Morning Glory)

Mimosa shared how her identity as a nurse kept her from getting the help she needed. "If somebody said, 'you need treatment.' I would say, 'Oh no, I don't. I'm a nurse. I know how to do this.'" Napeta declared, "I worked the whole time with short sleeves. I never put on long sleeves. I never tried to hide anything. So that [needle marks] was in plain sight and maybe that was the best-kept secret in the world because. . . It could not be . . . you know what I mean. It could not be me . . . I was not suspected."

Purple Lilly revealed:

We don't look like what they think drug addicts look like. Like I just met with my boss to ask for her to . . . and she said to me, "God I look at you and I just don't see it." And I just said to her, "it's because that's what we do." And there's a really important piece that when someone like me tells this story of the stuff I've done, and you look like you look and we judge by appearance. I have to learn to not always use, "I'm a nurse" as the first way I describe myself, it's a piece of me. But, it allows for a lot of rationalization for the behaviors that I had because people see nurses in the community as these angels and they wouldn't do that . . .You have a nursing degree, but underneath all of that, you have all of this stuff too. And that is not going to protect you from the consequences of these actions . . . I used being a nurse to keep myself sort of special and distant from other people. (Purple Lilly)

Heather also agreed. She's told others about her past and how she is, "a recovering alcoholic . . . I tell everybody . . . it helps me to smash that illusion that addicted women are living under the bridge or they become prostitutes or whatever. We're mothers, we're nurses, we're graduate students, whoever we are, we're everybody."

EMOTIONALISM, DEJECTION, AND THE NEED FOR SELF-CARE

When Heather became sober, she described needing to take time away from the profession. "I didn't work as a nurse for five years because I felt, I was totally depleted, I was just totally depleted by the time I got sober. There was not anything left inside of me that was of a good spirit, you know, totally depleted." Heather further explained, "Within our own profession we don't support our own . . . we eat our young . . . we tear them up. That is the foundation of nurses. It is perpetuated particularly in the hospital environment, in the acute care environment where you need teamwork."

Jasmine Jade framed it differently, "It's not that we eat our young, it's that literally nurses are bullied into their perfection and we're not perfect. We're far from it. We're very emotional, caring, loving people." Jasmine Jade passionately stated:

> You can't love anyone till you love yourself. We were giving away our skills, our knowledge, but never a piece of me and you have to have a separation in order to survive because we lose patients. The problem is, how do we teach nurses to have that healthy separation? We focus so much on our professional skills, knowledge, education, and maintaining the no-error mode. Nurses cannot make errors, then we get lost in perfection and we are not perfect, we are not perfect . . . the humanness goes, . . . and that was the other thing that nursing school, it empowered me; but, at the same time they gave me an unrealistic view as to how much I could affect someone else's life . . . You took it on, as if it was your fault, and that was the wrong way to do it. Had someone explained to me earlier on that "Hey . . . you do the best you can. Maintain within professional boundaries etcetera, but, when something goes wrong it is not your fault." This taking on the guilt for anything that may have happened, and a lot can happen in just one shift and that was the thing. I had no way to shed the guilt, other than drinking. Because supposedly it made you forget, but it really doesn't. (Jasmine Jade)

Jasmine Jade also noted further in her discussion her feelings of anger and dejection:

> It was the Board of Nursing threatening to take my license and I said, "Oh, no you don't get to have it. I will do what it takes," but you have to realize that there's a problem and you have to be teachable. I looked at it as this is part of the journey. I wasn't happy about it, don't get me wrong, I'm very human. I was angry at myself for a long time because I'd always been in sports, I was the MVP, team captain. At nursing school, I was a class president. I was always the one that everyone strived to be like and suddenly I was at the bottom of the barrel and nobody wanted to be like me. (Jasmine Jade)

Morning Glory exclaimed:

> I wanted help. I wanted a solution, but I didn't know what it was, and all that I could see that would help me was drugs and alcohol. I was so broken, yeah, and that's all I knew. And so, like you put me in intensive recovery, you force me to get everything that I had to get the hard way over a five-year period, and you give that to me concentrated in six months in an inpatient. Could it have been different? I think so. I wanted to survive. I wanted to get better. But, I tell you if the Board would have told me to do that, I would have done it, because nursing was everything to me. I want, I mean that's where I got, the only place I got joy, was by being a nurse. (Morning Glory)

DENIAL, SHAME, AND SECRECY
PERPETUATED BY THE STIGMA OF ADDICTION

Denial generally belongs to the person dealing with addiction, but it is also perpetuated by others. Napeta explained, "Denial is not a river in Egypt. Oh, no, it's, it is, if denial holds, you deny that you have to die. Oh no, it's powerful!" Purple Lilly described a significant incident where her family chose to ignore what was evident:

> I had a seizure at home the morning after I'd been using, I was on the phone with my mom and I had a seizure, and I was in the emergency room and did all this testing. I was up in my parents' house for two weeks. Everyone thought it was my eating disorder. Nobody, and the crazy part is, that I had a syringe on my bathroom counter and my sister saw it, and nobody asked me – not one person, not in the hospital, not in my family. They saw a syringe on my bathroom counter. I had a seizure, and nobody said, "Are you using drugs?"
>   The only thing I can think of is that the denial, they didn't want to see me as that person. It was hard, they just shut it out. I mean it's so shameful to admit this; but, I had this bag that I kept in my closet with all these syringes and old needles that I would take back to work to get rid of them because I'm a conscious [conscientious] drug addict. [Laughter] I'm at least going to get rid of my sharps in a sharps container. Right? My mom and my sister opened it and they asked me about it and I said, "Oh well that's from my ex-boyfriend and I just haven't you know, I just kept them cause I didn't know where to get rid of them." And I'm like, I'm a nurse and I don't know where to get rid of sharps? I was such a liar and they just were like, "Oh, OK, that makes sense." I mean it was to me it was so obvious. But even in the hospital nobody said, "Do you think she could have a drug problem?" "Do you think she drinks too much?" Or maybe they did, and my mom was like, "No, no, no," because there's a huge issue there too. (Purple Lilly)

Purple Lilly also talked about the shame of stealing drugs, "There's a level of shame that you carry when you know you've taken drugs from your job and you could have injured a patient, but you didn't. Only nurses who have done those things get the depth of what that feels like." Mimosa further described the shame nurses shared about accessing drugs on the job:

> We went to the city and went to nurses group there. My God, I sat in that group and for the first time, I heard something I hadn't heard in my recovery, and that is the professional part. I heard other nurses talking about their shame, what they had done. The stuff that should never be shared out loud at meetings, at AA and NA meetings, because it scares the public. (Mimosa)

Heather speaks of the impact of shame on nurses, "It's very hard to move from that place of shame, loathing, disgust and all that to a place where you say, okay, I'm not a bad person. I did not ask for this, but I am responsible for my recovery... I am working with nurses to help them move from this terrible place of guilt and shame that can paralyze you. It can paralyze you."

Jasmine Jade shared what happened when she approached her supervisor about her substance abuse problem:

> They don't want to know. Nurses with a history of alcoholism and addiction don't get to work. It all has to be a secret. Secrets make you sick. They force you to live a double life, basically . . . I've been terminated and then excommunicated, so I've just been stubborn and said, "You know, I'm a human being that made a mistake and I admit to it. I have accepted the consequences, and I have reformed and etcetera" . . . Nothing professionally, they've done nothing but try to crucify. Shall I say it was basically career suicide because I went originally to my boss and said, "I think I got a problem? Can you help me out?" (Jasmine Jade)

Mimosa described her life of secrecy:

> I couldn't wait to get home to have a drink. That was life . . . it was really on after I got married and I had to hide the drinking as much-- . . . [spouse] didn't know about the drugs . . . I wasn't a flower child. I was hidden . . . I had to start hiding it more. I was hiding the drug use from work, but now I had to hide my alcohol use. It couldn't be upfront . . . I always felt like it was a secret anyhow. (Mimosa)

Heather suggested that the actions of the healthcare industry perpetuated the shame and nurses hiding their substance use disorders:

> Only one . . . of all of the numbers of hospitals that stands by the nurse . . . The other facilities fire them right on the spot, irregardless of the number of years you have had at the hospital and not active in addiction. So that's a big issue. That's our own industry perpetuating the stigma. Yea, perpetuating the stigma. Their own nurses . . . Somehow, we became a throwaway part of the system. (Heather)

She further explained:

> I ended going back and getting a masters and I focused on women and substance abuse. And once again I was learning more about myself as well. The fact that more women die of cirrhosis than men, ten times as many women die of cirrhosis. The fact that women when they drink alcoholically from start to finish, they're lucky in 5, 10 years, their dead. The fact that there is still a terrible stigma about women alcoholics. There is a terrible stigma, social stigma, a community stigma. You know we think we're so advanced. We're not, there's a stigma. Now I am in recovery and I tell everybody. I am an alcoholic in recovery, because I've got nothing to be ashamed of. It took me twenty years though to get comfortable with that, but I am very comfortable with it. But there is a stigma. (Heather)

The participants all described how because they look a certain way and are educated, there is a misconception that they are immune to substance use disorders. They discussed how hiding substance abuse is perpetuated by the reactions of others in the healthcare industry. Because of the stigma, nurses who admit to drug and alcohol addiction are expendable and discarded, careers are ended.

Chapter Fifteen

Confrontational "Crisis" and the "Wake-up Call"

THE WAKE-UP CALL

Every participant shared a major event that happened to change the life course they were on. None of these seven nurses found recovery on their own. Jasmine Jade explained, "What happened was everything kind of came together in the perfect storm." Mimosa disclosed how her addiction led to an emergency situation in the hospital where she was working:

> I created a crisis while working in . . . surgery department . . . I took too much, a detail man from a drug company came by and he brought—I told him that I really could use something, it was called Furanol. He gave me a whole bottle of Furanol . . . anyhow I couldn't walk and talk really good after taking too many then . . . I liked it. He gave me a whole bottle, oh God, and I wound up in this neurological collapse, supervisor took me up, laid me down and called my husband and said, "Come and get her." They took me to . . . Hospital and . . . They did all—I let him do all kinds of test on me . . . I wasn't going to tell them. That's what I call it. I created a crisis that's stopped it. Because I could have (died) . . . and then while I was sitting there, this lady came at me with this big syringe and I knew they're going to do a tox screen here. I knew the jig was up . . . and the doctor was angry with me. . . and the doctor came in and scolded the hell out of me. He just really let me have it and I was so ashamed already. (Mimosa)

Morning Glory disclosed:

> Because the first thing that happened was I got caught. You know at work and they said you can go into Diversion and of course I wanted to keep my nursing license. So, I went into Diversion; but Diversion was not enough for me.

That's just my story. . . . I mean I relapsed after a couple months. I had to go to inpatient. Then I got out of inpatient, I couldn't I was, I couldn't stay sober, so I tried to kill myself, I no longer ... Diversion wasn't enough, but Diversion pointed me to Alcoholics Anonymous. And what I needed was other alcoholics who had gotten sober. So that's what I needed. (Morning Glory)

Purple Lilly described that after she successfully completed the Diversion Program (a five-year process), dental work led to relapse and job loss:

I mean from day one like you do just pick up where you left off and then I had dental work and I had this prescription for Percocet and that's when I was just off and running and I was thinking when I got that filled "I don't think I am going to need 30 of these Percocet." They give me 10 Valium and 30 Percocet for one dental procedure and all in the back of my mind I thought, "I need to tell someone that I have this," but then I thought, "but I don't want to because then someone's going to take it away and I'm not going to be able to use it the way I want to use it." And pills were never my thing. But then they became like a great substitute. And then what happened was I ran into my old boss and he was dumb enough to offer me a job again.

I hadn't, I could not bring myself to face him and make amends. So, in the office that day, as he's offering me a job, I am half-assing making the amends. "That was way back it's not going to happen again," and he's like, "I know . . . I know it was just something you were going through," and there had been other nurses that worked at this place that had gone through Diversion, and the lack of education is just crazy to me. But, I also know that I'm very convincing and when I tell someone, "no," like I can make you think that everything's fine. So, I went back to work there and within a week, I was diverting again; within three, I lost my job— No, not even 90 days . . . never thought I would be back at that job putting Demerol in my pocket again. I went into that fully convinced that I had it all under control, and this was going to be my living amends, and everything was going to be fine. And three months later, I crashed and burned. (Purple Lilly)

Rose explains how she relapsed while on Board of Nursing probation and she had a moment of reckoning to find true sobriety:

They just told me that I was going to be—I would get notice whether I was accepted or not into probation. I got a letter. I'm accepted into probation. They told me it's three years. I can apply after two for early release and then the mandates, the testing and meetings, the group. I got back into it. That was in . . . I started relapsing and I remember just feeling this, is it. You're going to get caught. You're going to lose your license . . . Now at this point then I was asking this woman in AA for her urine, she is giving it to me because I would make up stories all the time just such a schemer, God! Then in . . . I had to go for a test and I was positive, and she wasn't really responding to me because she had talked to her sponsor and her sponsor deleted me from the gratitude list and obviously told her not to do it, which is a good thing, and of course I was resentful.

Off I go down to the office and I was positive, and the office was closed down and I had called them earlier in the day to see what time they are open until, because I was going to come down after work. I did have some urine with me. It was really cold. I didn't realize that at time that they had put me on a watch list. Yes. I don't know what happened, but they were going to put me in and watch (observe) me do it, because they hadn't been doing that on probation. They were (observing) in Diversion. The whole office was shut down. I called my probation monitor and I told . . . "the office is closed down, they said 'we were going to be open.'" And *(probation monitor)* said "I'm going to have you get proof of that that you had an appointment, send it in, this is going to be considered a missed test and it's going to be considered a mark against you." That's it and *(probation monitor)* said, "Usually three marks and you're out." Yes, it scared me and actually as I was walking away from that lab, I had a moment of reckoning with myself. "You know what *(name, Rose)* your kind of a loser, look at you. You've got this urine in your pocket. You're running around scheming . . ." and I remember . . . the judge too had a profound effect to me . . . because he gave me a chance. He saw something in me, I didn't see in myself. That was another thing I was thinking about. I was thinking about *(nurse facilitator)*, how *(nurse facilitator)* doesn't mess around.

Then that was it. I did what *(nurse facilitator)* said. You get a sponsor. You go to meetings. You do the steps. You're honest. You're open. You're willing. Step one, two, three. Yes. Just do it. Of course, the addict mind was talking saying "just do it for two years and then you can tell them this didn't work for me, thank you, goodbye," but it happened. I got sober for real . . . That almost happened to me (death) with the cocaine. I was taking enough of a dose at that point that I would pass out. It's crazy . . . You go into this robotic mode, it's very bizarre. You can't stop it . . . Now, I have a good relationship with my higher power, I think. He puts people in my life like *(nurse facilitator)*. (Rose)

Napeta explained how substance abuse was finally recognized by others and the relief it provided:

I was out of plans and again, so I fall flat on my face which was, the face went, was one of the best things ever happened. Of course, I didn't know it at that moment. When a friend called me from . . . I mean somebody I went to nursing school with, so I know this guy for, 40 something years. He comes over and . . . He said, "I'm just asking just a clerical question. How are you doing?" And so, in a sense, in that moment of clarity. I said, "oh you want to know how is it going?" and I relayed it, what I was doing. *(At this point, Napeta paused, his voice broke and he became tearful and wiped his eyes)*. That's so powerful because he started crying and I'm like. . . He's started crying . . . So, I asked why he started crying. He was afraid of losing somebody he loves and so then he asked me, "Does anybody know?" I said, "no, you are the first one." He said, "Why don't you do this" – critical work. "Go to the cafe and call a shrink." He was saying the same things, what I was thinking; but I needed to hear it from the outside in order to act upon it. And that was like a revelation, still . . . today. (Napeta)

According to Napeta that was the first of multiple wake-up calls:

> These two managers had lunch together . . . then they put two and two together
> and then actually went into Pyxis which is known as the dispensing system.
> And they put my name in and then they said, "Oh my God." They changed the
> Pyxis after that in the hospital. So, then it came all out. So, then she called me
> in for some paperwork which was true. But when I came in she said, "(*name
> Napeta*) we have to talk." We went out to the Nursing Supervisor's office
> there, and there was HR sitting there and the doctor sitting there, two managers
> so they were all there. In that sense I know, the gig was up . . . I said, "okay
> just ask me." And I was also happy and relieved that I could tell, and of course
> broke down and cried. (Napeta)

Mimosa's comments summarized these experiences, "Alcoholics and addicts are always causing 'crisis' and it gets old. This was mine and I feel like my higher power knew how to get me where I needed to be. That's part of my story. It's a wake-up call." Purple Lilly articulated that the "wake-up call" was required because they needed to be caught!

> Telling people if you have a problem ask for help? That's the stupidest thing I
> ever heard, because nobody with a problem, unless you're desperate, and then
> you've gotten to a point where it's probably too late. And there are conse-
> quences when you ask for that like that. "Oh God, please help me." The prayer
> of desperation. But to say to someone, "I'm stealing drugs and I really would
> like help." That's not realistic. Maybe one out of a thousand people are going
> to do that and the rest of us are going to wait until we get caught! (Purple Lilly)

ESSENTIAL INTERVENTION BY MANAGERS AND SUPERVISORS

Purple Lilly spoke about the importance of noting suspicious behavior and the need for employer intervention, "I think employers are scared and there needs to be like this open dialogue around. If we see anything suspicious, we're going to call you on it because our job is to protect your patients, and whether it turns into nothing, fine."

The need for hospitals and medical centers to verify access to substances was represented in the story previously shared from Napeta and was further evidenced in the public state discipline records for Morning Glory, where it was noted that in one 10-day period, she diverted over 60 doses of Hydromorphone from the Pyxis machine for her own use:

> I go in because I'm trying to pick up a shift, so I can get drugs. I'm desperate. I
> mean I didn't even need the money; I was making so much money. And so I, I
> go in and they float me because I am the per diem so I'm the last on the list. So
> I float to the Tele floor, Med Tele and so I was like shit, because I worked on
> oncology where there's lots of pain meds. I was like, damn it. What am I going

to do? And so I'm freaking out. I need opiates. I need it. And that's my first priority. That's all I'm thinking about. I'm not thinking about the patients I need to take care of, or the work I need to do.

And I go in and I look at my patients that I'm picking up in that shift. And none of them have any opiates prescribed to them. And I'm scared and I'm freaking out. I'm desperate. So, then I just start scrolling through all the patients in the Pyxis which is the drug machine and I see another nurse's patients, patient has I think, probably Demerol or Dilaudid I think it was, no it was Dilaudid. And so, I just take some out. And this f*** nurse . . . she is the type of nurse. There's not that many who go in, she goes in and does the reconciliation of everything that's been taken out during her shift because she was the shift before me. She sees that I just took out some Dilaudid and she comes and confronts me, "Hey," and I don't even know her because I floated to this floor. She's like "hey, why did you just take Dilaudid out on my patient?" And I was like "oh he just told me, I was walking by and he complained of pain." You know I lied. So, she went right to her manager and I had already gone in the bathroom and used it. And so, she told her manager. They already had some data on me because I'd been taking excess stuff. They said, "you can't start your shift." (Morning Glory)

Morning Glory continued, "They took me to a room. My manager came from my floor, the manager from that floor, the head pharmacist, they all confront me you know, and they're mean and tough because they, they don't want me to deny it. And I immediately started crying and said, 'I know I know this is wrong. I know,' oh my God, you know. *(She became teary eyed as she speaks).* So, I admitted to everything, immediately."

Rose revealed that being fired was devastating:

Then that was kind of the end at that point. That was kind of the end because– how did it all go down? It went down. I was still taking Dilaudid as well. Somehow it was noticed that it was taken out in the morning and given to a patient and the patient said they didn't get it . . . In the morning, yes, before my shift started that I had given it to a patient, and the patient said that she didn't get it. I pulled it out under her name in the morning. I was on day shift at that time. They confronted me . . . the charge nurse. I actually can't remember what I said and then that whole day they allowed me to work. I had taken it. It wasn't really as effective, it was more kinda, just like I felt tiny, but more normal . . . just to be normal. I worked that day and I knew I was in trouble, but they let me work. I think they didn't know what to do. They pulled me into a room they said that, "You took it out under here and you gave it to the patient? The patient said, 'they didn't get it.'"

No, I didn't confess. I made up an excuse I can't remember what. Then they called me and told me not to come to work. Then they brought me to HR a couple of days later. I was devastated. I was very low, very devastated . . . and when I called the Board of Nursing . . . she told me, the intake nurse for the Diversion program, "This is the best thing that could happen to you and you probably don't feel like that's true. But believe me," she said, "It is," so I remember that. Then they took me, they told me about the Diversion program. They told me I didn't have a job with them anymore. They reported me to the board and that was that. It was the end of 2006 when I was fired. (Rose)

Purple Lilly's manager tearfully confronted her about her drug diverting after she was given a second chance and subsequently relapsing:

They were on to me a little bit faster this time. Like, I think they started to see the behaviors, and I could sense there was a different energy. And one day a Fentanyl went missing and like just weird things started to happen now that (*name Purple Lilly's*) back and so they got all their evidence together and I will never forget on... coming into work and they sort of like interfered and brought me in the office and he was like, he was bawling crying. I devastated that man. And I, it was, I mean it was the worst day of my life. (*Purple Lilly got teary eyed*) And he said, "I just like," he felt like he had failed me because "we didn't set up some type of a safety net." There was a lady in Diversion who got out who was still being randomly drug screened and why they didn't offer that to me, I don't know, but I think because they wanted to give me the benefit of the doubt. I don't know. (Purple Lilly)

Every participant shared, in every interview, how some major crisis or event was necessary for them to become sober. They had to have some type of confrontation and intervention by employers, family, or friends to break from their escalating substance abuse. Almost every participant became tearful when expressing the humiliation, disappointment, and hurt they and others experienced during the confrontation. The greatest fear for all of them was they would lose their nursing career.

Chapter Sixteen

Recovery: Spiritual Awakenings and Recovery Communities

Often overlooked, it's the spiritual component in that program too. Not just realize the physical and psychological. It also has that spiritual component which is in a sense like one of the essence and that is defined by each person, themselves, I mean it's spiritual, but not religious. Someone can choose their own little, how they want to deal with that because that aspect may be sometimes, be detrimental to the people because it's a non-entity so that is like one thing which should also, I think, not be overlooked. It's important. (Napeta)

SURRENDER AND HEALING

Jasmine Jade described surrender as one of the most powerful" important moments in her recovery:

I'll never forget the day that I surrendered and that was when I knew I had to go to the hearing in June and probation was supposed to begin. The moment I surrendered was that night before June 1st, [my family member] was eight months old and she was sleeping with her head in my lap and I had a glass of wine in front of me, I just looked up and I said, "God, I can't do this alone. Please help me." That was it, I never had the desire to drink again. (Jasmine Jade)

Napeta described recognizing his "red flag" as his moment of surrender:

And again, that moment sitting there that was not my . . . I didn't think that was my finest moment. But, actually it was and so, therefore, very often, I keep that in mind because I always have my little red flag which you know, if I get too cocky, too self-confident, sarcasm is not good in a difficult situation. I have that flag in my head to check in with myself and I always remind myself

that was my greatest moment, the moment of surrender. I looked up surrendered until I found the definition in recovery, which I like, which means
crossing over to the winning side. (Napeta)

Heather elaborated on the steps she took in her recovery:

When I was five years sober, I went back to make amends to my last employer
because she was grooming me for big things. She was a very nice director of
nurses and I just really, I did her dirty. That's what you do when you become a
drunk. I went back. I went back to her in . . . and I said, "I am so sorry. But I
want you to know, I am an alcoholic. I am in recovery. My behavior to you
was impertinent, it was disrespectful." I just did my amends. I just took out my
laundry list and I did it. She came from behind her desk. She hugged me. We
both cried and then she offered me a job in their chemical dependency unit—
go figure. (Heather)

Napeta clarified that the difference between sobriety and recovery is that
recovery requires going through the painful process of continuous rehabilitation:

I mean. That is where the people who survive or who go for it. They're not
[just] dry . . . No, it's really embracing it and going through all the pain all the
different levels through all these layers of onions which are peeled away.
Which you know if you ever peeled an onion you know there's a lot of crying
involved, obviously more emotional and depth there in order to (sish) . . . "Oh,
I got that somewhat in check" and then (sish). Issues are like tissues another
sneaks in. You pull one and you think you're done, and oops there's another
one, oops and it only stops when the box is empty, so that means when you
die.
    I need to have readjustment of who am I, what am I, how. And it's a long
laborious process that in a sense it's the same as addiction. You know if I do
the same thing, my sponsor told me in the beginning, I only have to go to
meetings on the days where I used to drink. So, for me that meant daily . . .
when people ask me, "Are you still going to the meeting? Are you still engaged?" Because nobody asked me, "Oh you still have to go to the bar? You
still have to whatever order beer or have champagne on Christmas Eve and on
birthdays do this, that and the other." It's only one life to live . . . very often
substance abuse is self-medication. And it helps one get through life to a
certain extent until it turns on oneself. (Napeta)

Jasmine reflected:

Well, the way I keep it going is maintain my prayer, my gratitude, positive
attitude. Also, I try, whenever possible, I go to AA meetings to remind me how
quickly things can change. Also, the Board of Nursing forced me-to do relapse
prevention courses. I still have the book, so whenever I get a little edgy, I
believe in the HALT: happy, angry, lonely, tired; then you need to be alert.

Keep a clear head. "This too shall pass" is a real good attitude to have when things are looking like, "Okay, a drink's looking pretty good right now" . . . This too shall pass. (Jasmine Jade)

SPIRITUAL RECKONING AND MOMENTS OF CLARITY

Finding a greater power in people and in a spiritual presence appeared to support these nurses in their recovery. Heather, drawing on decades in recovery, explained:

I tell everybody I am a recovering alcoholic. I do that because I want people to realize that there is recovery and that it does happen. And my own personal, I so believe that if there is any word I could share with ... nurses is it's not your fault. But now that you know you're an addict, you are responsible for your recovery... It's a miracle. And how it has affected me in my life is, today, I am the person, I always wanted to be. I am not the star of the show. I am not in control of the universe. I am the person I always wanted to be, and I am the person my God wanted me to be. Okay – That's all and I do the best I can in this role. So, I think it has completely changed my life in so many ways, so, so many ways. I've learned to live in the present moment, that's a miracle. (Heather)

Heather further elaborated:

The grace that happened to me continues to happen to me on a daily basis and like I said, I live in the present. I've learned how to love other people. I've learned how to receive their love. I've learned how to have compassion for my nurses my friends. I never had all that and it's all grace. It's grace because I did not do this. It's a grace that I had a wake-up call and got sober and staying sober for today. So, I think that is one of the greatest gifts I have in my life is to know this is a gift and it is a fragile gift, a fragile, fragile gift. So, I am grateful, I am grateful to have this for the hard times as well as the great times. Cause it's the hard times that would throw me back out there. I have developed a support system that is so healthy that it keeps me healthy. (Heather)

Rose similarly acknowledged, "I have a good relationship with my higher power I think. He puts people in my life. Yes. God filled up the spiritual hole. I had a spiritual awakening in step 10." Jasmine Jade shared how having a relationship with God was key to her rebirth:

I was missing the joy of life. I was giving joy to people and patients, I was giving, giving, giving, but I was not receiving. That's what you have to learn, you have to have that balance of you give so much of yourself to your family, at home, at work everywhere, but what are you receiving? That's the whole point of the rebirth when it comes to having a relationship with God. You allow God to come into your heart and it's the same thing with our careers. (Jasmine Jade)

She further described her spiritual connection:

The best part is I came freely with all my raw materials I have collected in my life. I can name a few, sadness, helplessness, powerlessness, pain, loss, anger, loneliness. The people at this church greeted me with open arms and a warm embrace. I did not feel threatened or insignificant. In fact, I felt something deep within me. That lightened my heart. I can explain only that I no longer felt like the tiny flame in a powerful wind storm struggling to remain burning in a lantern on a rocky ship. [laughter] That was my life. Intense! I understand from the first handshake and warm embrace *you* do not have to do it, nor do you have to do it alone. These words are very simple. It had triggered an ocean of curiosity which has begun rivers of thought I never knew existed. I had been awakened with a child-like awe excited, and eager to turn another page in this amazing life. (Jasmine Jade)

SOBRIETY CHALLENGES AND THE "GIFT OF RECOVERY"

Getting sober and staying sober, according to the participants, have many challenges. Morning Glory explained her first attempt at sobriety:

There's stuff going on. And I'm home I have no job and I'm trying to just do recovery you know. And I look back, I could've just dove in and I didn't know how. I was shut down. I was so closed off to people. And I could have gone into meetings and reached out and created a community and I just didn't know how. I don't, I look back and I wish I knew how that could have been different for me. (Morning Glory)

Napeta also explained:

Getting sober in a sense is difficult. But it's not that hard. Staying sober is a difficult thing because life still comes at me or at us in the same speed and I can't change that. It's an outside source. I only can change my attitude and perception towards that. So, that means my reaction to my first thought I can control, as much as control is elusive. So, maintaining that is what actually grows and all the years what is happening, is actually that time buys some time. That means if I'm going to create the moment, then I have a little bit more, hopefully, time to react and to draw on some experience. (Napeta)

Jasmine Jade also declared, "I was determined to get back because I knew I had reformed. I knew that I was rehabilitated. I knew I didn't want that life anymore because I was introduced to a much better way of life." Heather also joyfully proclaimed, "To me, the greatest gift to my life is that I have 32 years: not only sober, but in recovery. And that foundation has allowed me to be a fabulous grandmother." Jasmine Jade further revealed how recovery helped her get her joy back:

> He (*nurse support facilitator*) scared me in the beginning, but it was a good scare. Because he said, "You have two options you can live, or you can die. Which would you like?" Basically, and I was like "What are you talking about?" We are in such denial. I was angry, trust me, I was one angry nurse when all that started happening. Then I had to take a look at me and my behavior and I was a professional "What are you talking about?" "Not me." It was very humbling. I used to think being the smartest, the fastest, the quickest, the most energetic, the prettiest, all of that seemed to matter until I went to recovery and I realized that nothing matters, if you don't have your sanity. If your perception is warped because of substance abuse, stress, poor misman-agement, not appropriately or coping effectively with a positive outcome. Then you miss the joy, so the greatest impact is that I got my joy back. (Jasmine Jade)

Heather revealed:

> I eventually went back and got by bachelor's degree in nursing. And the only reason I became interested in alcoholism is because I became an alcoholic and my fall into this disease was a very rapid fall. Within 5 years I lost everything. Five years— it was a very fast ride from 'you know' social drinking to prob-lem drinking to alcoholic drinking to daily drinking to losing my marriage, losing my daughter, leaving nursing. What saved me was I left nursing. I opened a flower shop [laughter] "hello" you see. But it was the grace that did that, it was not me, it was the grace. But after I got sober . . . after losing everything and I also lost my ability to be a nurse. And I was very aware of the fact. I didn't have the Board of Nursing telling me anything. The winners would tell me, "you're not quite ready to back to nursing kid. I don't want you taking care of me."
>
> But, at that point I had finished my bachelor's degree in nursing and I ended up taking classes at . . . in alcoholism and addiction. I just took classes, but it was for me and I found out that, and this was over time, this was not something that happened quickly, I found out that I had no vote as to whether or not I was going to be an alcoholic—no vote. What I had a vote in was whether I was going to do recovery so that's where my energy went. I was very active in alcoholics anonymous, two meetings a day. I had a sponsor, I sponsored other women. And I took this class so that I could learn about alcoholism. And at this point now in the 80's we were talking addiction was a disease. I had to learn that. Because, like most women, who have a problem with alcoholism or drugs, my shame was eating me alive. My shame was eating me alive! And so, when I went to these classes and I took, you know I became like a certified something or other, but I took like a year and a half of classes all about alcoholism, learning all about the disease. (Heather)

Purple Lilly offered, "We get so attached to what we do and how we define ourselves, but I mean it's the best decision I ever made was to become a nurse and I'm so happy that I did. I certainly have . . . made some decisions that it could have turned out much differently. The fact that I'm still a nurse is a gift."

ESSENTIAL PERSONAL AND COMMUNITY SUPPORT SYSTEMS

All the participants shared their gratitude for the support systems within the recovery community. Heather stated, "For me personally, the biggest support system was Alcoholics Anonymous [AA]." Jasmine Jade also recognized her church and AA:

> My support systems were the church and AA. The Board of Nursing was not a support system. They were the ones who had the power to end it all, end my career. I respected them, and I followed their rigorous program . . . I met through one of the guys, because I said, "I'm an RN on probation and I need a sponsor." That's how I began. "I don't care anything about your AA. I have to get a paper signed, Board of Nursing forced me to come here. I need a sponsor." And then through that sponsorship, three years, I learned trust. I learned how to talk. Going through the steps taught me how I could cope effectively. It began to nurture that innate ability that I had to begin with. It was recipe. One, two, three, four, five that became the recipe for nurturing my ability to cope with life, effectively without having to turn to alcohol or anything that was mind consuming. It's good to read books on recovery, it's good to interact with people in recovery, it's good to attend meetings in recovery and also volunteer your services. Be part of the community because you only get out of recovery what you put into it. There's nothing for free, you have to want it. (Jasmine Jade)

Morning Glory expressed that the Board of Registered Nursing's Intervention (Diversion) program was an important factor in directing her to the organization best suited to support her recovery:

> Diversion helped me a lot. It pointed me to Alcoholic Anonymous. I have a sponsor who I talk to all the time, who is like my mom. It's just like I have a family now that are all people who are in recovery. So that's what it is. It's people. That's the whole basis of Alcoholics Anonymous. It's one alcoholic helping another. That's recovery right there. (Morning Glory)

According to Heather:

> I'm a great believer in, nurses particularly, we need outside professional help. Not everything is going to be resolved in AA. So, we need professional outside help. And we need it from a professional that understands recovery. They have to understand recovery. And they have to understand that nurses, our middle name is codependent. So, they have to have a background in those areas in order to be beneficial to us. I remember when I first went into therapy. So, I

went into therapy. I remember the therapist said to me, "So what are your needs...?" So, I said "I don't have any." [Laughter] I was 46 years old, 46. "I don't have needs." How sick is that? Huh. [Laughter] "Oh, I don't have needs. I got this." (Heather)

Additionally, Morning Glory described the value in seeing the same people and becoming part of a community:

I mean I found the healthiest people outside of nursing with the best recovery, let's say. You don't have to go to NA. Because a lot of NA groups are you know junkies that have been on the street and nurses can't relate, first priority is community. I need to go to the same meetings, see the same people multiple times a week and become part of a community. That is the most important thing, that's how I learned, that's how I had people in my life calling me on stuff. I wanted to be like them. And so, I kept seeing them and talking to them. (Morning Glory)

Mimosa elaborated on key steps in her recovery process:

First of all, physical sobriety came first, and when you feel better, physically, you can get into the spiritual and emotional recovery. Then, the fourth step in AA, doing the Inventory step, and then sharing it with a sponsor, or with whomever you trust well enough to share some of this stuff, just really helped me begin to look at my behaviors and how I thought, and how I acted. And of course, all I had was what I was given from childhood, and here I am, 29 -- at that time, not now – [Laughter] and I'm just learning how to live and thank God! (Mimosa)

Purple Lilly similarly described her recovery process focusing on the importance of staying attached:

I think part of the first process was that day I was in the office with my boss and being willing to leave there and call my friend and ask for help, and actually get a sponsor and do what was suggested. And I think one day when I realized not that I fully get recovery, because I think it's a lifelong process, and sometimes I feel like I get it and sometimes I don't. So that's why I have to stay connected. But I have these old thoughts of, "Wow, I don't want to tell that person that I'm going to this place to do this thing." What is that about? I can now see where I would hide in my life and I choose not to hide today and that to me is recovery, actively recruiting people in my life that are also in recovery that keeps me accountable, so that when I try to start drifting off and isolating, they're like "No I think we should go for coffee and yoga" . . . We all do that for each other and I just think the willingness to be open to let people in is when you know you've entered into recovery.

None of this, I got on my own. I only know these pieces about myself because somebody was gracious enough to bear with me through all of these steps and through this process to allow me to see that this is who I am. And they drug me kicking and screaming to meetings, the young people's meetings on Friday night and out to dinner afterwards. They literally just took me under their wing and they're like, "This is what we do here" when I go to nurse support group, I'm like, oh these are my people because there's an understanding that I don't have to explain it to anyone else. (Purple Lilly)

Finally, Napeta noted the importance of connection and being a part of the recovery community and programs:

It's referred to as a link in the chain, so you should be a link in chain so that you have somebody who you in a sense look up to or ask for advice or "Cry me a river," who has more time than I do. My sponsor has 25 years, then I have of course people who I have shown the way, what AA is and so that my sponsors, which I have right now which are in constant contact, and then going to meetings socializing is very important to receive empathy and compassion levels. Then after those meetings being engaged with newcomers to a certain degree. Then having the people in your, it's called a home group. It's a group where you go to no matter what. I choose a Man's meeting so that I don't have any distractions because it's about recovery in there and not about socialization. It's also a book study because the big book of AA is like a workbook, so you read it and then you reread it and reread it. And you highlight, and you work with it. So, every time you read it you find different aspects of it depending on the mood or the insight you have at that moment.

Then, one of the big things for me is like meditation, being in the moment. I mean not just in the morning but doing it throughout the day like because the moment is the only thing we have. Everything else is speculation. Everything else is past. So, I can learn from the past that not to repeat that behavior or mistakes or whatever its experiences. Learn from that and then apply that to the now. That is how I obtain and maintain my recovery and sobriety and how I rely on it. (Napeta)

Most of the participants shared that a spiritual awakening led them to embracing not just sobriety, but recovery. They said it was the support of the recovery community that educated them about substance use disorders, its addictive power, and their continual vulnerability. They believe it is essential to be a part of a supportive network and to stay a part of the recovery community. This support is vital to their continued recovery!

All the participants in this study had substance use disorders somewhere in their family history. This impacted how they viewed drugs and or alcohol in their early developing years, which continued and usually magnified in nursing school or early in their nursing career, maybe as a result of their individual risks for using substances and the lack of education around substance abuse issues. It was not addressed in their lives until a major catastrophe, event, or crisis took place. They all experienced the shame, denial, and stigma of the disease and were at times blinded to their issues, not just by the denial processes of the disease, but also by the nursing identity and the misconception that exists within the profession that nurses are immune to addiction.

The participants all indicated how nursing is important to them; however, they had to learn how to cope with life in new ways. These ways were presented to them by the recovery community and personal support systems established by the community. They all indicated how recovery now is the "gift" that helps them daily be the best of themselves: sober, caring, and having new healthy relationships and a new joy of living.

VI

THE DISCOVERIES:
RESULTS AND INTERPRETATIONS

Chapter Seventeen

Five Major Results

The findings were drawn from the voices of seven registered nurses and were analyzed to become the themes and subthemes. There were five major results or discoveries that emerged out of the nurses' voices. These discoveries are considered in relation to theory, research, and practice. These findings and themes informed the results for this study, which were discussed in relation to prior research on nursing and substance abuse. As outlined in previous section, the five main themes that emerged from the experiences of the participants were: (a) family dynamics and patterns; (b) substance use disorders in nurse education and within the nurse profession; (c) illusions and secrets of the nurse professional; (d) confrontational "crisis" and the "wake-up call;" and (e) recovery, spiritual awakenings and recovery communities. The results that were generated as a product of these themes are outlined in this chapter.

RESULT ONE—FAMILY HISTORY AND PATTERNS OF EARLY ALCOHOL AND DRUG USE "SET THE STAGE" FOR LATER SUBSTANCE USE DISORDERS

The participants in this study indicated that family history played a major part in their early use and abuse of drugs and alcohol. They grew up in families where alcohol or drug abuse was present, and their home environment influenced how they viewed substance use. These early experiences may have led them to grow up with "pharmacological optimism,"[1] believing that substance use was an acceptable way to change their emotional state.[2] Being raised in a family with a history of alcoholism, drug use, emotional impairment, or emotional abuse frequently resulted in low self-esteem, overwork, and overachievement, suggesting that these individuals are at greater risk for substance use and abuse.[3]

Additionally, many of the participants were high achievers. They either had advanced degrees or leadership positions and or worked in areas where they had major responsibilities. One participant continued her drug abuse while she attended graduate school and throughout her advanced practice. This is consistent with the literature that suggests substance-abusing nurses often have challenging positions, are considered high achievers, have advanced degrees, graduate near top of their classes, have great admiration and respect from their colleagues, and come from families that have one or more parents who are substance abusers.[4] The participants shared how their positions and the respect colleagues, family, and community had for them allowed them to rationalize their substance use and hide the severity of their disease. This aligns with findings that nurses with these backgrounds may have a set of implicit biases identified as "justification of mechanisms of addiction" to justify their substance use.[5]

Four of the participants indicated they knew they were different around alcohol or drugs and were immediately affected at an early age by the sensations surrounding its use. They continued to seek out these sensations throughout their nursing career. This reflects conclusions that there are significant differences in the sensation-seeking behaviors between those who have a family history of abuse and others who do not.[6] The participants stated that although the alcohol use or drug use made them sick or black out, they knew they would continue to seek that sensation again and again.

RESULT TWO—WORKPLACE STRESS AND ACCESS WITHOUT APPROPRIATE SELF-CARE TRAINING AND EDUCATION ABOUT SUBSTANCE USE DISORDERS NEGATIVELY IMPACT THE NURSING PROFESSION

All the participants in the study revealed they started using and abusing drugs and alcohol either before or in nursing school, and the substance use continued throughout their careers. All the participants indicated that while in nursing school, they received little to no training about substance use disorders as it relates to nurses. None of them were made aware of their own risks for a substance use disorder or how substance abuse is an occupational hazard for those within the nursing profession. Studies have confirmed that substance use and abuse by nurses usually begins before or while they are in school and is not sufficiently addressed by the nursing profession.[7] There is a gap in the education of nursing students regarding their risks of substance use disorders.[8]

Many of the participants indicated they originally worked in high stress areas while using. Participants explained how they liked the adrenaline rush they received from working in some of the high stress units. Previous research has shown that stressful working conditions, experiences, access to the prescriptions, and education regarding prescription drugs contribute to the potential for a nurse's addiction.[9]

All of the nurses in the study had some degree of identifiable risk factors for drug abuse. These risk factors are: (a) family history, (b) early experimentation of drugs and/or alcohol, (c) unusual attitudes regarding substance use and abuse, (d) lack of education, (e) stress, and (f) workplace access. Yet, despite all these risks, the nursing schools and their employers had inadequate policies, response mechanisms, and substance abuse training to manage these identifiable influences that afflict the nurse and jeopardize the profession.[10] These risks were further compounded by their assumed knowledge and education on the effect of drugs, the frequency they administered drugs, their relative ease of access to drugs, and their lack of apprehension.[11]

These participants' experiences indicated there was a lack of self-care and a denial and illusion by the nurses, their family, coworkers, and others that they, as nurses, were not easily susceptible to substance abuse. Nurse coworkers and family members continued to ignore several signs and symptoms that occurred in the lives of the participants indicating they had a problem. This illusion is perpetuated within the nursing community and has its historical significance borne from the Florence Nightingale model, a model specifying nursing traits: dedication, self-sacrifice, and abstinence from alcohol and drugs.[12] One participant stated she did a "lot of rationalization for the behaviors" because "people see nurses in the community as these angels and they wouldn't do that [drugs]." This participant is correct, as public polls currently and consistently rank nurses the highest of all professions in trust and ethical standards.[13] This nurse image, of continual giving and self-sacrifice and a lack of appropriate coping mechanisms, enabled many participants to hide and justify their continual abuse of prescription drugs, alcohol, and opiates.

RESULT THREE—THE STIGMA SURROUNDING SUBSTANCE USE DISORDERS HINDER NURSES FROM ACKNOWLEDGING THEIR ADDICTION AND MANAGERS FROM PROVIDING NECESSARY SUPPORT

Although alcoholism and addiction are recognized by the American Medical Association and the American Nurse Association as diseases,[14] the participants did not feel this has been sincerely carried into the nurse professional's workplace. One participant indicated that any progress made because of the early declarations surrounding the disease of addiction has eroded and is no longer being emphasized. Six of the participants were adamant about the stigma they felt existed towards them or those in the nurse profession because of their substance use disorder. They described how they were "throwaway nurses." This is corroborated by research indicating, society continues to see "addiction" as a moral issue and lack of willpower and not a "brain disease" with increasing stigma on females.[15] This stigma comes from a long history in which "addicts" were seen as "fiends"[16] and considered "useless, dangerous and amoral and immoral beings."[17] The participants expressed their belief that many of these attitudes still plague the nursing profession.

As a result of several issues surrounding addiction, for years these participants concealed their substance abuse. Although research indicates that nurses usually work for approximately five years with a substance use disorder before their addiction is discovered,[18] these participants were able to practice nursing and conceal their alcohol and or drug use for an average of 19 years. Whether this was the result of the stigma, lack of education, lack of awareness by coworkers, shame, or denial, they were unable to acknowledge their disease, which ultimately jeopardized patient safety.

There is another component to addiction that prevents nurses from acknowledging their abuse. This component is the extremely powerful effect drugs have on the brain. All the participants declared how they were powerless to the demands of their addiction. They at times shared how much they wanted to stop using but could not. They did not know how or did not have the inner ability to resist the urge. This aligns with the research regarding substance abuse, recognizing that addiction is a disease that is destructive, progressive, and persistent despite all consequences.[19] Every one of the participants expressed how he or she was powerless and a victim of the disease. One participant confessed how she had gained sobriety and was convinced she "had [her addiction] under control" and within one week she was putting "Demerol in her pocket again" and within 90 days she "crashed and burned." This is consistent with addiction research that insists the major characteristic of addiction or a substance use disorder is an individual's willingness to continue with behaviors that are self-destructive or self-defeating despite the consequences to the individual's quality of life.[20] The person who is addicted has the tendency to regard their life decisions and patterns as uncontrollable.[21] This individual sees herself (himself) as a victim plagued by and powerless to resist the recurring onslaught of compelling urges.[22]

Additionally, in several instances when the participant nurses reached out for help, they were, as one nurse described, "excommunicated, . . . crucified" by those she reached out to. Another stated, when her addiction was discovered, and she needed help, she was, "discarded." Several nurses expressed feelings and observations that nurses are easily "expendable" and seen as "costs" and not "revenue." They shared how there was little support for them once their addiction was discovered. This reaffirms conclusions that there is no encouragement for nurses to show concern and speak up in support of one another and there is not a culture of safety in hospitals.[23] This is of grave concern since nurses are the largest group of healthcare providers with the most access to patients and patient medications.

RESULT FOUR—A "CRISIS" OR "WAKE-UP-CALL" IS NECESSARY TO PROVIDE THE TRANSFORMATION OR MOMENT OF RECKONING NEEDED TO JOLT A NURSE OUT OF ADDICTION INTO RECOVERY

The participant nurses needed a wake-up-call or crisis by forces outside him or herself before they got sober and entered recovery. This wake-up can lead them to a moment of reckoning or spiritual awakening. All the participants were forced into sobriety by a personal confrontation or crisis. Two participants indicated it was a physical crisis that got them started in recovery. Three participants admitted they were caught at work and confronted, while two others had personal confrontations with family or friends or the criminal justice system. These all were types of intervention necessary to halt their addictive behavior. Interventions are confrontational and traumatic, yet they are crucial as the first step in the process of assisting a substance-abusing nurse. In each incident when the participants described the situations that occurred—the trauma, embarrassment, relief, and shame—they became tearful and reflective. This confirms that an intervention for both those doing the intervening as well as the suspected substance abuser, can be one of life's most traumatic events.[24] The added consequence for some of the participants was they were immediately terminated, not reported to regulatory agencies timely, and not provided any treatment support. Some hospitals, for the safety of the patients, have a zero-tolerance policy and only immediately terminate the nurse. Although this may appear, on the surface, to be useful and the appropriate reaction, this policy can contribute to addiction stigma and does not serve the public. If the nurses are aware that this is the ultimate reaction to their disease, they will engage in greater activities and go to greater lengths to conceal their disease when they are hired at other facilities. These types of policies do not provide any support to the nurse, they only help them minimize and rationalize their disease and drives their substance abuse issues further underground.[25]

Additionally, one of the participants expressed the trauma of the confrontation and how at one point she attempted to commit suicide and was surprised she survived her incident. Without proper identification, intervention, and treatment, the trauma of confrontations and loss can result in a confronted nurse becoming suicidal; therefore, the nurse's safety should be considered and he or she should not be left alone during any "intervention or post-intervention process."[26] However, when there is the proper support by and concern from individuals within the community, many times nurses can have a monumental change and "moment of clarity" in their lives. Several of the participants explained how they had a "spiritual awakening," "moment of reckoning," and or "moment of clarity" when they were confronted and especially when those confronting them were genuinely concerned about their well-being. This allowed them to look at themselves with clarity. These types of moments confirm several studies that suggest early intervention, education, and dealing with the substance use in a positive manner assists the nurse and provides a better opportunity for the nurse's rehabilitation and recovery.[27]

RESULT FIVE—NURSE ADDICTS CAN RECOVER AND LEAD SOBER AND PRODUCTIVE LIVES IF THEY ARE PART OF RECOVERY COMMUNITIES TO WHOM THEY ARE ACCOUNTABLE

The first step to sobriety for the participants was the intervention they experienced. However, they acknowledged the difficulty is not just getting sober, it is staying sober. They had to undergo some type of treatment to maintain their sobriety and enter recovery. Studies confirm that effective treatment is the first step to recovery.[28] For some of the participants, it took multiple attempts at treatment before they were able to maintain sobriety. Two of the participants were mandated by the BRN to enter extensive inpatient treatment. One was successful, and the other participant admitted she was able to convince the BRN she could complete her treatment by doing a less intense outpatient treatment. She now admits she was wrong. She did not stay in the inpatient treatment long enough. She believes had she remained, she would not have relapsed and been terminated out of the Board's Diversion (Intervention) Program, which ultimately led to her license being revoked. Research confirms that when treatment is sufficiently intense, matches the needs of the client, and is followed by continued therapeutic support systems, it is effective and successful.[29]

The participants shared that a powerful aspect of their recovery programs is that they teach you how to cope with life and live differently. They disclosed how the personal support in AA, the Board's Diversion (Intervention) Programs, and the Nurse Support Groups they attended taught them how to look at life differently and how to manage situations. They declared how the self-efficacy taught in AA was one of the most important tools they needed. Many also explained how the Nurse Support Groups were essential in allowing them to express their shame, humiliation, and pain to others within their profession that understood. Research validates their experiences, explaining that the treatment that encourages self-efficacy with skill-building activities like stress management training and coping skills training have the best recovery outcomes.[30]

Three of the participants shared how their whole identity was tied up in being a nurse. They learned through AA that they had an identity outside of nursing. Many divulged how they were able to do restitution and pay back entities for their cost and their behavior. There is "an extensive body of scientific evidence" indicating that healthcare professionals do particularly well in specialized treatment when addiction is approached as a treatable disease.[31]

Recovery transforms lives. All the participants expressed they had a great life transformation when they decided to take their recovery seriously and do the treatment programs step-by-step. They all realized at some point that recovery is more than just being sober. One participant reiterated that getting sober is not difficult, it is staying sober. He emphasized that it takes being in a recovery community for that to happen. Another participant declared that an individual may not have control on becoming an addict; however, she was adamant that an individual does have control over his or her recovery. Other participants stressed the importance of staying accountable to the same home group or support group that sees you consistently.

Many studies also declare that recovery is more than just the absence of use.[32] It takes on many forms and behaviors and is a lifestyle change. Those in recovery recognize that substance use disorders are problematic and need to be avoided. Additionally, the participants stressed the importance of having healthy relationships within their support systems. They identified how their personal and community support systems kept them connected and accountable. They all expressed the importance of a spiritual connection to their higher power and how this connection made a difference. Several participants described how a hole was filled in their lives by recovery and their higher power. This connection is essential to their recovery. This is in alignment with other studies that indicate the importance of reconnecting with healthy and nourishing relationships, such as family, twelve step groups and a higher power and disassociating with alcohol and drugs.[33] Additionally, self-acceptance, self-care, and coping are important parts of reconnecting.[34]

NOTES

1. A. M. Trinkoff et al., "Workplace Access, Negative Prescription, Job Strain, and Substance Use in Registered Nurses," Nursing Research 49, no. 2 (2000): 83.

2. J. M. Brewster, Drug Use among Canadian Professionals (Ottawa, Canada: Minister of National Health and Welfare, 1994); M. Buxton, "Three-Step Recovery Model Aids Impaired Nurses," Hospital Employee Health 1 (1982); Trinkoff et al., "Workplace Access, Negative Prescription, Job Strain, and Substance Use in Registered Nurses."

3. G. Monahan, "Drug Use/Misuse among Health Professionals," Substance Use & Misuse 38 (2003).

4. J. O. S. I. E. O'Quinn-Larson and M. R. Pickard, "The Impaired Nursing Student," Nurse Educator 14, no. 2 (1989).

5. J. L. Bowler, M. C. Bowler, and L. R. James, "The Cognitive Underpinnings of Addiction," Substance Use & Misuse 46 (2011): 1061–62.

6. M. M. West, "Early Risk Indicators of Substance Abuse among Nurses," Journal of Nursing Scholarship 34, no. 2 (2002).

7. M. A. Boulton and L. J. Nosek, "How Do Nursing Students Perceive Substance Abusing Nurses?," Archives of psychiatric nursing 28, no. 1 (2014); B. Heise, "The Historical Context of Addiction in the Nursing Profession: 1850-1982," Journal of Addictions Nurse 14, no. 3 (2003); T. Monroe and F. Pearson, "Treating Nurses and Student Nurses with Chemical Dependency: Revising Policy in the United States for the 21st Century," International Journal of Mental Health and Addiction 7 (2009); T. B. Monroe, "Addressing Substance Misuse among Nursing Student: Development of a Prototype Alternative-to-Dismissal Policy," Journal of Nursing Education 8 (2009); National Council of State Boards of Nursing (NCSBN), "Substance Use Disorder in Nursing, a Resource Manual and Guidelines for Alternative and Disciplinary Monitoring Programs," (2011), https://www.ncsbn.org/SUDN_11.pdf.

8. Monroe and Pearson, "Treating Nurses and Student Nurses with Chemical Dependency: Revising Policy in the United States for the 21st Century;" D. Murphy-Parker and R. J. Martinez, "Nursing Students' Personal Experiences Involving Alcohol Problems," Archives of Psychiatric Nursing 19, no. 3 (2005); National Student Nurses Association (NSNA), "Resolution: In Support of Nursing School Policies to Assist and Advocate for Nursing Students Experiencing Impaired Practice," in National Student Nurses Association (Philadelphia, PA: NSNA House of Delegates, 2002); D. Quinlan, "Impaired Nursing Practice: A National Perspective on Peer Assistance in the U.S.," Journal of Addictions Nursing 14, no. 149–155 (2003); G. H. Rassool and S. Rawaf, "Predictors of Educational Outcomes of Undergraduate Nursing Students in Alcohol and Drug Education," Nurse Education Today 28 (2008).

9. Heise, "The Historical Context of Addiction in the Nursing Profession: 1850–1982;" R. Martinez, "Innovative Roles Executive Director of Peer Assistance Services: An Interview with Elizabeth M. Pace," Journal of Addictions Nursing 13, no. 1 (2001); P. Zickler, "Nida Scientific Panel Reports on Prescription Drug Misuse and Abuse," National Institute on Drug Abuse Notes 16, no. 3 (2001).

10. M. Haack, "Stress and Impairment among Nursing Students," Research in Nursing and Health 11, no. 2 (1988); Monroe, "Addressing Substance Misuse among Nursing Student: Development of a Prototype Alternative-to-Dismissal Policy;" S. Murphy, "The Urgency of Substance Abuse Education in Schools of Nursing," ibid.28 (1989).

11. S. Luck and J. Hendrik, "The Alarming Trend of Substance Abuse in Anesthesia Providers," Journal of PeriAnesthesia Nursing 19, no. 5 (2004); Trinkoff et al., "Workplace Access, Negative Prescription, Job Strain, and Substance Use in Registered Nurses;" A. M. Trinkoff, C. L. Storr, and M. P. Wall, "Prescription-Type Drug Misuse and Workplace Access among Nurses," Journal of Addictive Diseases 18, no. 1 (1999).

12. O. Church, "Sairey Gamp Revisited: A Historical Inquiry into Alcoholism and Drug Dependency," Nursing Administration Quarterly 9, no. 2 (1985); Heise, "The Historical Context of Addiction in the Nursing Profession: 1850-1982;" E. F. Pollard, Florence Nightingale: The Wounded Soldier's Friend; Fully Illustrated, (London: S. W. Partridge and Co. Ltd., 1911), http://hdl.handle.net/2027/uc2.ark:/13960/t3qv3tp56; J. G. Widerquist, "The Spirituality of Florence Nightingale," PDF only, Nursing Research 41, no. 1 (1992).

13. A. M. Gallup, ed. Gallup Poll: Public Opinion 2009 (Blue Ridge Summit, PA: Rowman & Littlefield Publishers, 2010).

14. National Council of State Boards of Nursing (NCSBN), "Substance Use Disorder in Nursing, a Resource Manual and Guidelines for Alternative and Disciplinary Monitoring Programs;" National Institute on Drug Abuse (NIDA), Drug Abuse and Addiction: The Basics, (2016), http://www.drugabuse.gov/publications/media-guide/science-drug-abuse-addiction-basics.

15. S. Trossman, "Issues Update: Nurses' Addictions," The American Journal of Nursing 103, no. 9 (2003): 27.

16. M. I. Wilbert, "The Number and Kind of Drug Addicts," Public Health Reports (1896–1970) 30 (1915): 2290.

17. M. Singer and J. B. Page, The Social Value of Drug Addicts: The Uses of the Useless (Walnut Creek, CA: Left Coast Press, 2013), 17.

18. D. Booth and A. Carruth, "Violations of the Nurse Practice Act: Implications for Nurse Managers," Nursing Management 29, no. 10 (1998).

19. G. F. Koob and M. Le Moal, "Addiction and the Brain Antireward System," Annual Review of Psychology 59 (2008).

20. Bowler, Bowler, and James, "The Cognitive Underpinnings of Addiction."

21. Ibid.

22. J. Balmford and R. Borland, "What Does It Mean to Want to Quit?," Drug and Alcohol Review 2008, no. 27 (2008); J. Mendelson and N. Mello, The Addictive Personality (New York: Chelsea House, 1986); J. A. Schaler, Addiction Is a Choice (Chicago, IL: Open Court Publishing, 2000).

23. N. Darbro, "Alternative Diversion Programs for Nurses with Impaired Practice: Completers and Non-Completers," Journal of Addictions Nursing 16, no. 4 (2005); D. Maxfield et al., "Silence Kills–the Seven Crucial Conversations for Healthcare," Vital Smarts (2005).

24. R. H. Coombs, Drug-Impaired Professionals (Cambridge, MA: Harvard University Press, 1997).

25. National Council of State Boards of Nursing (NCSBN), "Substance Use Disorder in Nursing, a Resource Manual and Guidelines for Alternative and Disciplinary Monitoring Programs;" Quinlan, "Impaired Nursing Practice: A National Perspective on Peer Assistance in the U.S.."

26. National Council of State Boards of Nursing (NCSBN), "Substance Use Disorder in Nursing, a Resource Manual and Guidelines for Alternative and Disciplinary Monitoring Programs." 251.

27. R. A. Eller and B. L. Irwin, "Responding to the Chemically Dependent Nursing Student," Journal of Nursing Education 28, no. 2 (1989); G. E. LaGodna and M. J. Hendrix, "Impaired Nurses: A Cost Analysis," JONA: The Journal of Nursing Administration 19, no. 9 (1989); National Council of State Boards of Nursing (NCSBN), "Substance Use Disorder in Nursing, a Resource Manual and Guidelines for Alternative and Disciplinary Monitoring Programs."

28. T. B. Monroe et al., "The Prevalence of Employed Nurses Identified or Enrolled in Substance Use Monitoring Programs," Nurse Research 62, no. 1 (2013); National Council of State Boards of Nursing (NCSBN), "Substance Use Disorder in Nursing, a Resource Manual and Guidelines for Alternative and Disciplinary Monitoring Programs."

29. A. T. McLellan et al., "Drug Dependence, a Chronic Medical Illness: Implications for Treatment, Insurance and Outcomes Evaluation," Journal of the American Medical Association 284 (2000); National Institute on Drug Abuse (NIDA), Drug Abuse and Addiction: The Basics.

30. M. Ilgen, J. Mckellar, and R. Moos, "Personal and Treatment-Related Predictors of Abstinence Self-Efficacy," Journal of Studies on Alcohol and Drugs 68 (2007).

31. National Council of State Boards of Nursing (NCSBN), "Substance Use Disorder in Nursing, a Resource Manual and Guidelines for Alternative and Disciplinary Monitoring Programs." 2.

32. J. Blomqvist, "Recovery with and without Treatment: A Comparison of Resolutions of Alcohol and Drug Problems," Addiction Research & Theory 10, no. 2 (2002); A. B. Laudet, "What Does Recovery Mean to You? Lessons from the Recovery Experience for Research and Practice," Journal of Substance Abuse Treatment 33 (2007); R. Margolis, A. Kilpatrick, and B. Mooney, "A Retrospective Look at Long-Term Adolescent Recovery: Clinicians Talk to Researchers," Journal of Psychoactive Drugs 32, no. 1 (2000).

33. C. Masters and D. S. Carlson, "The Process of Reconnecting: Recovery from the Perspective of Addicted Women," Journal of Addictions Nursing 17 (2006).

34. L. G. Payne, "Self-Acceptance and Its Role in Women's Recovery from Addiction," ibid.21 (2010).

BIBLIOGRAPHY

Balmford, J., and R. Borland. "What Does It Mean to Want to Quit?" *Drug and Alcohol Review* 2008, no. 27 (2008): 21–27.

Blomqvist, J. "Recovery with and without Treatment: A Comparison of Resolutions of Alcohol and Drug Problems." *Addiction Research & Theory* 10, no. 2 (2002): 119–58.

Booth, D., and A. Carruth. "Violations of the Nurse Practice Act: Implications for Nurse Managers." *Nursing Management* 29, no. 10 (1998): 35–39.

Boulton, M. A., and L. J. Nosek. "How Do Nursing Students Perceive Substance Abusing Nurses?" *Archives of psychiatric nursing* 28, no. 1 (2014): 29–34.

Bowler, J. L., M. C. Bowler, and L. R. James. "The Cognitive Underpinnings of Addiction." *Substance Use & Misuse* 46 (2011): 1060–0.

Brewster, J. M. *Drug Use among Canadian Professionals.* Ottawa, Canada: Minister of National Health and Welfare, 1994.

Buxton, M. "Three-Step Recovery Model Aids Impaired Nurses." *Hospital Employee Health* 1 (1982): 24–27.

Church, O. "Sairey Gamp Revisited: A Historical Inquiry into Alcoholism and Drug Dependency." *Nursing Administration Quarterly* 9, no. 2 (1985): 10–21.

Coombs, R. H. *Drug-Impaired Professionals.* Cambridge, MA: Harvard University Press, 1997.

Darbro, N. "Alternative Diversion Programs for Nurses with Impaired Practice: Completers and Non-Completers." *Journal of Addictions Nursing* 16, no. 4 (2005): 169–86.

Eller, R. A., and B. L. Irwin. "Responding to the Chemically Dependent Nursing Student." *Journal of Nursing Education* 28, no. 2 (1989): 87–88.

Gallup, A. M., ed. *Gallup Poll: Public Opinion 2009.* Blue Ridge Summit, PA: Rowman & Littlefield Publishers, 2010.

Haack, M. "Stress and Impairment among Nursing Students." *Research in Nursing and Health* 11, no. 2 (1988): 125–34.

Heise, B. "The Historical Context of Addiction in the Nursing Profession: 1850–1982." *Journal of Addictions Nurse* 14, no. 3 (2003): 117–24.

Ilgen, M., J. Mckellar, and R. Moos. "Personal and Treatment-Related Predictors of Abstinence Self-Efficacy." *Journal of Studies on Alcohol and Drugs* 68 (2007): 126–32.

Koob, G. F., and M. Le Moal. "Addiction and the Brain Antireward System." *Annual Review of Psychology* 59 (2008): 29–53.

LaGodna, G. E., and M. J. Hendrix. "Impaired Nurses: A Cost Analysis." *JONA: The Journal of Nursing Administration* 19, no. 9 (1989): 13–18.

Laudet, A. B. "What Does Recovery Mean to You? Lessons from the Recovery Experience for Research and Practice." *Journal of Substance Abuse Treatment* 33 (2007): 243–56.

Luck, S., and J. Hendrik. "The Alarming Trend of Substance Abuse in Anesthesia Providers." *Journal of PeriAnesthesia Nursing* 19, no. 5 (2004): 308–11.

Margolis, R., A. Kilpatrick, and B. Mooney. "A Retrospective Look at Long-Term Adolescent Recovery: Clinicians Talk to Researchers." *Journal of Psychoactive Drugs* 32, no. 1 (2000): 117–25.

Martinez, R. "Innovative Roles Executive Director of Peer Assistance Services: An Interview with Elizabeth M. Pace." *Journal of Addictions Nursing* 13, no. 1 (2001): 49–51.

Masters, C., and D. S. Carlson. "The Process of Reconnecting: Recovery from the Perspective of Addicted Women." *Journal of Addictions Nursing* 17 (2006): 205–10.

Maxfield, D., J. Grenny, R. McMillan, K. Patterson, and A. Switzler. "Silence Kills–the Seven Crucial Conversations for Healthcare." *Vital Smarts* (2005): E5.

McLellan, A. T., D. Lewis, C. O'Brien, and H. Kleber. "Drug Dependence, a Chronic Medical Illness: Implications for Treatment, Insurance and Outcomes Evaluation." *Journal of the American Medical Association* 284 (2000): 1689–95.

Mendelson, J., and N. Mello. *The Addictive Personality.* New York: Chelsea House, 1986.

Monahan, G. "Drug Use/Misuse among Health Professionals." *Substance Use & Misuse* 38 (2003): 1877–81.

Monroe, T. B. "Addressing Substance Misuse among Nursing Student: Development of a Prototype Alternative-to-Dismissal Policy." *Journal of Nursing Education* 8 (2009): 272–77.

Monroe, T. B., H. Kenaga, M. S. Dietrich, M. A. Carter, and R. L Cowan. "The Prevalence of Employed Nurses Identified or Enrolled in Substance Use Monitoring Programs." *Nurse Research* 62, no. 1 (2013): 10–15.

Monroe, T., and F. Pearson. "Treating Nurses and Student Nurses with Chemical Dependency: Revising Policy in the United States for the 21st Century." *International Journal of Mental Health and Addiction* 7 (2009): 530–40.

Murphy, S. "The Urgency of Substance Abuse Education in Schools of Nursing." *Journal of Nursing Education* 28 (1989): 247–51.

Murphy-Parker, D., and R. J. Martinez. "Nursing Students' Personal Experiences Involving Alcohol Problems." *Archives of Psychiatric Nursing* 19, no. 3 (2005): 150–58.

National Council of State Boards of Nursing (NCSBN). "Substance Use Disorder in Nursing, a Resource Manual and Guidelines for Alternative and Disciplinary Monitoring Programs." (2011): 280.https://www.ncsbn.org/SUDN_11.pdf.

National Institute on Drug Abuse (NIDA). *Drug Abuse and Addiction: The Basics.* 2016. http://www.drugabuse.gov/publications/media-guide/science-drug-abuse-addiction-basics.

National Student Nurses Association (NSNA). "Resolution: In Support of Nursing School Policies to Assist and Advocate for Nursing Students Experiencing Impaired Practice." In *National Student Nurses Association* Philadelphia, PA: NSNA House of Delegates, 2002.

O'Quinn-Larson, J. O. S. I. E., and M. R. Pickard. "The Impaired Nursing Student." *Nurse Educator* 14, no. 2 (1989): 36–39.

Payne, L. G. "Self-Acceptance and Its Role in Women's Recovery from Addiction." *Journal of Addictions Nursing* 21 (2010): 207–14.

Pollard, E. F. *Florence Nightingale: The Wounded Soldier's Friend; Fully Illustrated.* London: S. W. Partridge and Co. Ltd., 1911. http://hdl.handle.net/2027/uc2.ark:/13960/t3qv3tp56.

Quinlan, D. "Impaired Nursing Practice: A National Perspective on Peer Assistance in the U.S." *Journal of Addictions Nursing* 14, no. 149–155 (2003).

Rassool, G. H., and S. Rawaf. "Predictors of Educational Outcomes of Undergraduate Nursing Students in Alcohol and Drug Education." *Nurse Education Today* 28 (2008): 691–701.

Schaler, J. A. *Addiction Is a Choice.* Chicago, IL: Open Court Publishing, 2000.

Singer, M., and J. B. Page. *The Social Value of Drug Addicts: The Uses of the Useless.* Walnut Creek, CA: Left Coast Press, 2013.

Trinkoff, A. M., Q. Shou, C. L. Storr, and K. L. Soeken. "Workplace Access, Negative Prescription, Job Strain, and Substance Use in Registered Nurses." *Nursing Research* 49, no. 2 (2000): 83–90.

Trinkoff, A. M., C. L. Storr, and M. P. Wall. "Prescription-Type Drug Misuse and Workplace Access among Nurses." *Journal of Addictive Diseases* 18, no. 1 (1999): 9–16.

Trossman, S. "Issues Update: Nurses' Addictions." *The American Journal of Nursing* 103, no. 9 (2003): 27–28.

West, M. M. "Early Risk Indicators of Substance Abuse among Nurses." *Journal of Nursing Scholarship* 34, no. 2 (2002): 187–93.

Widerquist, J. G. "The Spirituality of Florence Nightingale." PDF only, *Nursing Research* 41, no. 1 (1992): 49–55.

Wilbert, M. I. "The Number and Kind of Drug Addicts." *Public Health Reports (1896-1970)* 30 (1915): 2289–94.

Zickler, P. "Nida Scientific Panel Reports on Prescription Drug Misuse and Abuse." *National Institute on Drug Abuse Notes* 16, no. 3 (2001): 1–5.

Chapter Eighteen

Foundational Elements to Recovery

Previous studies indicated there are three foundational elements to recovery: First is identifying the life-threatening aspect of substance abuse. Second is maintaining abstinence. Third is developing the support programs to maintain sobriety.[1] Additional foundational elements were developed as the result of this research. According to this study, the participant's journey took them through five elements of recovery: First, an outside force jolted them into sobriety. Second, they identified the life-threatening aspect of substance abuse and the harm it was causing around them. Third, they each surrendered and had a spiritual moment and or moment of reckoning or clarity by acknowledging something was missing and they could not stay sober alone. Fourth, they were able to maintain their abstinence. Finally, all the participants were adamant about the importance of their personal and community support programs as a part of maintaining their sobriety. This is confirmed by the research that shows that social supports systems, especially large support networks, potently impact the ability of individuals to remain abstinent.[2]

The participants acknowledged that they have many individuals within different aspects of the recovery community to whom they are accountable. They realized they could not become sober and stay sober without the support of sober individuals who reached out to them and showed them how to live a new life of recovery and wholeness. The participants described how they were either "awakened" or "forced" into recovery through circumstances or "dragged" kicking and screaming to meetings. Yet, the process worked. When they surrendered, the "miracle happened" and they discovered a new healthy lifestyle.

The participants provided personal information related to their journeys to recovery, which were life-changing experiences. They admitted they could not have perceived what being in recovery was like prior to getting sober. All the participants acknowledged that sobriety and recovery is not a journey one can do alone. It takes a community of love and support and it is continuous.

NOTES

1. J. F. Kelly et al., "A 3-Year Study of Addiction Mutual-Help Group Participation Following Intensive Outpatient Treatment," *Alcoholism: Clinical and Experimental Research* 30 (2006); M. J. Landry, *Understanding Drugs of Abuse: The Processes of Addiction, Treatment and Recovery* (Washington, DC: American Psychiatric Press, 1994); National Council of State Boards of Nursing (NCSBN), "Substance Use Disorder in Nursing, a Resource Manual and Guidelines for Alternative and Disciplinary Monitoring Programs," (2011), https://www.ncsbn.org/SUDN_11.pdf.

2. J. Witbrodt et al., "Day Hospital and Residential Addiction Treatment: Randomized and Non-Randomized Managed Care Clients," *Journal of Consulting and Clinical Psychology* 75 (2007); K. Witkiewitz and G. A. Marlatt, "Relapse Prevention for Alcohol and Drug Problems: That Was Zen, This Is Tao," *American Psychologist* 59 (2004); W. H. Zywiak, R. Longabaugh, and P. Wirtz, "Decomposing the Effects of Social Networks Upon Alcohol Treatment Outcome," *Journal of Studies on Alcohol and Drugs* 63 (2002).

BIBLIOGRAPHY

Kelly, J. F., R. Stout, W. Zywiak, and R. Schneider. "A 3-Year Study of Addiction Mutual-Help Group Participation Following Intensive Outpatient Treatment." *Alcoholism: Clinical and Experimental Research* 30 (2006): 1381–92.

Landry, M. J. *Understanding Drugs of Abuse: The Processes of Addiction, Treatment and Recovery.* Washington, DC: American Psychiatric Press, 1994.

National Council of State Boards of Nursing (NCSBN). "Substance Use Disorder in Nursing, a Resource Manual and Guidelines for Alternative and Disciplinary Monitoring Programs." (2011): 280. https://www.ncsbn.org/SUDN_11.pdf.

Witbrodt, J., J. Bond, L. A. Kaskutas, C. Weisner, G. Jaeger, D. Pating, and C. Moore. "Day Hospital and Residential Addiction Treatment: Randomized and Non-Randomized Managed Care Clients." *Journal of Consulting and Clinical Psychology* 75 (2007): 947–59.

Witkiewitz, K., and G. A. Marlatt. "Relapse Prevention for Alcohol and Drug Problems: That Was Zen, This Is Tao." *American Psychologist* 59 (2004): 224–35.

Zywiak, W. H., R. Longabaugh, and P. Wirtz. "Decomposing the Effects of Social Networks Upon Alcohol Treatment Outcome." *Journal of Studies on Alcohol and Drugs* 63 (2002): 114–21.

VII

CONCLUSION AND RECOMMENDATIONS

Chapter Nineteen

Conclusion

The purpose of this narrative research study was to give a voice to nurses who have experienced the effects of substance use and abuse in their personal and professional lives. The researcher sought to explore the greater insights and knowledge shared by nurses in recovery who have and are successfully dealing with their substance use disorder. The study sought to identify from their stories, these nurses' understanding of substance abuse and how the systems of support within their healthcare settings hindered or helped them address their personal substance abuse issues. The previous findings, results, and interpretations are the foundations for these conclusions and recommendations.

Seven participants, all registered nurses in California, participated in this narrative study. One participant was male and six were female. Two were born and raised in a foreign country where they completed most of their nursing education and all were Caucasian. Based on self-reports, these individuals described substance abuse for 6 to 27 years while they practiced nursing and before they entered recovery. The participants were from socioeconomic backgrounds ranging from lower middle class to upper class. Three of the seven participants have been formally disciplined by the State of California due to their behaviors related to substance abuse.

Six of the participants were interviewed on three separate occasions; one participant was interviewed in two interviews due to health restrictions. Through this process five themes emerged from the voices and experiences of the participants: (a) family dynamics and patterns; (b) substance use disorders in nurse education and within the nurse profession; (c) illusions and secrets of the nurse professional; (d) confrontational "crisis" and the "wake-up call;" and (e) recovery, spiritual awakenings, and recovery communities. The findings and results that emerged form the basis for the conclusions that follow. The findings, results, and conclusions frame the recommendations for nursing educators, nurse administrators, and others regarding how the systems of support within healthcare settings can be developed to support nurses dealing with substance use and abuse.

Substance use and abuse in nurses is an extremely complex phenomenon. It is viewed, researched, experienced and treated, through several different paradigms. It is a phenomenon that impacts nurses' lives in ways than can cause a great deal of pain and suffering. The conclusions are outlined in response to the three overarching research questions that framed this study. The research questions were developed to help the researcher identify, through the lived experiences of registered nurses, the challenges they faced, and the system supports available to them.

WHAT STORIES DO NURSES TELL ABOUT THEIR PERSONAL EXPERIENCES WITH SUBSTANCE USE AND ABUSE DURING VARIOUS STAGES OF THEIR CAREER?

All the participants in this study revealed how they have been greatly impacted by substance use and abuse in their personal lives and in their careers. They all shared that they had some degree of family history, and each described early experimentation (ages 11-20) with drugs and alcohol, little or no education about the potential challenges presented by access to drugs in the work setting, and that workplace stresses may have led to their addiction. Every participant described that they started or increased drug use while in nursing school. This use escalated while they were practicing registered nurses. It appears that the lack of formal training in both nursing school and subsequent professional development opportunities regarding how drugs influence moods may have minimized awareness of both the participants and those with whom they worked and allowed them to conduct patient care while under the influence.

Many of the participants shared how they gravitated to nursing practice in high stress units and in highly stressful situations. Some of the participants disclosed that they were *addicted* to the adrenaline rush, but all declared emphatically that they loved their profession and enjoyed caring for patients. Many of the participants stated they viewed their ability to work as a nurse as a special gift. Several of the participants shared how within their units they were highly respected and trusted by their coworkers. They sadly acknowledged, however, that as they progressed in their disease, they exploited and manipulated that trust. Many confessed they deceived, lied, and manipulated medical records, family, coworkers, and others to hide their disease and continue using their substance of abuse.

Most of the participants explained how the illusions that surround the professional image of "the nurse" allowed them to easily continue in their addiction despite any obvious signs or symptoms they were displaying. Their prestige as a nurse, the way they presented themselves, and the denial that existed among family and coworkers, and even their own self-deception, prevented them from seeing the full extent of their drug abuse and acknowledge the destruction drug use was causing in their lives. Some of the participants confessed they specifically chose to work in areas, such as emergency, surgery, and oncology units. This was an intentional way to feed their addiction, as it was relatively easier to access medications in these units. These participants further explained how their cravings drove them to diverting and using these drugs at home and even while at work. This led to personal shame, denial, misconceptions, and hiding. Yet, despite all this, they evidenced a belief that they were called to nursing for the greater good it offers to others. They believed they were caring people and were victims caught in an uncontrollable web of denial, lying, hiding, shame, and even grandiosity that was destroying their lives.

Several participants shared how they had physical crises at home and or at work as a result of their drug use and with various outcomes. There were incidents in which participants reached out for help and were disregarded or rejected because the nursing managers did not know how to handle nurses with substance use disorders. Three of the nurses discussed how they were disciplined by the Board of Registered Nursing (BRN) for their use and or diverting, while one nurse had her license revoked for two years.

The participants expressed they tried to stop their abuse to no avail or despite consequences. They shared how they felt they were the victims of the disease and they knew they were wrong; however, each was compelled to continue in their addiction despite their own misgivings. All feared losing their ability to work as a nurse, which caused them to hide their disease rather than come forward, as they were aware of the stigma of addiction within the nursing profession. Their behaviors continued until personal crisis situations occurred that forced them into sobriety and recovery.

They all emphasized they had to get caught to get sober, emphasizing they could not get sober alone. It took a major health crisis or work intervention to stop the trajectory of their disease cycle. Additionally, a few of the participants described that they experienced relapses and it took multiple interventions and multiple attempts at sobriety before they became stable in their sobriety and entered a life of recovery. These relapses caused grave consequences in their personal and professional lives, consequences such as near-death experiences, a time-limited loss of nursing license, and the possible loss of nursing careers.

WHAT STORIES DO NURSES, WHO
HAVE SUCCESSFULLY DEALT WITH SUBSTANCE USE
DISORDERS, TELL ABOUT THEIR RECOVERY?

The participants acknowledged that recovery was not easy, and it took hard work. According to the participants' stories, recovery started from a major confrontation in the work setting. It was expressed that it was unrealistic to believe someone in the throes of addiction will voluntarily stop using and come forth on their own without some major crisis. One by one, they shared how someone intervened to change the course of their journey, which, for most of the participants after the initial confrontation, started with a moment of reckoning or a moment of clarity. They stated they all had to go deep within and get clarity, look at their situation, look at their behavior, and recognize where they were headed. The participants shared how this was painful and had an element of suffering. Even in their explanation regarding their confrontations and spiritual renewal, the participants became tearful and reflective.

There were elements of loss the participants revealed that they had in relation to their self-esteem, nursing careers, and even their drug of choice. Each of these participants indicated they were initially devastated by addiction and the behaviors and consequences of the disease. They acknowledged that this experience with devastation helped get them to sobriety and eventual recovery. They revealed how those moments are now seen by all of them in one form or another as the best moments in their recovery journey.

Several participants shared that through their suffering, they attained new spiritual awakenings and revelations. They indicated their lives now have a purpose that goes beyond nursing. However, they all understood that their disease is right there waiting for them to make a misstep. The participants' shared that the gratefulness, joys, insights, and lessons learned through their individual journeys from addiction to recovery helped them navigate their lives.

HOW DO NURSES DESCRIBE THE SYSTEMS OF SUPPORT
WITHIN THE HEALTHCARE SETTING THAT HELPED
THEM ADDRESS THEIR SUBSTANCE USE DISORDER?

Most of the participants stated they were surprised how little support or information was provided in nursing school regarding substance use disorders and how to cope with stress in the workplace. They also described that they received little support from their employers when they reached out for help or when their addiction was discovered. Many believe there is a great stigma about drug use due to the singular focus on patient safety that exists in the healthcare setting. Only one participant described both initial and ongoing support from her employer, despite her relapse and mishandling of the second opportunity she was given.

Based on the findings in this study, it appears nurses receive very little education about substance access, work stress, and substance abuse, either in nursing programs or professional training. Hence, there is little preventive information provided by the nursing profession that assists nurses with understanding the addiction process and their own individual risks for abuse.

For most of these nurses, there were no systems of support within their individual healthcare settings. It was only upon referral to the Board of Registered Nursing's (BRN) programs and the outside recovery systems that exist that they were supported toward behavior change and eventual recovery. They shared how nurse support groups and AA support programs were two of the most significant programs that supported them in recovery. One participant shared how it was the love of church members in addition to the support programs that allowed her to change her life. For five of the participants, it was the BRN that directed them to these support programs. The other two participants discovered support programs through other nurses.

All the participants declared it was the programs that taught them about substance use disorders and recovery, not the nursing profession. They stated that the support programs gave them the tools to cope with stressful situations and helped them have a purpose and a new way to look at life and situations. The participants revealed it was through the recovery process and with the help of others with similar experiences that they became the people and nurses they were intended to be. All declared that, as a result of their recovery journey, they are better as nurses and as individuals.

All the participants ascertained that it was the people within these support programs that made the greatest impact in their lives. They were adamant that being accountable to a particular group and seeing the same people week after week was essential and made the greatest difference and impact in their recovery. The participants explained that those who had gone through addiction and were in recovery mentored them: they were tough on them, aware of the traps that could occur, and held them accountable. They described how at times they still have the desire to return to drugs, recognize that addiction is powerful and tricky, and that they must stay connected to others in recovery to remain in recovery.

The participants were adamant that being part of a recovery community is vital to their success. The participants with the extensive years of recovery shared that they were still committed to their AA support groups and continued to attend, despite their many years of sobriety, indicating that these support systems were a major reason they have succeeded. All the participants described recovery as a "gift," and some as a very "fragile gift!"

Chapter Twenty

Recommendations
and Final Observations

RECOMMENDATIONS FOR NURSE EDUCATORS, ADMINISTRATORS, AND HEALTHCARE AGENCIES

This study illuminates the serious lack of education, information, and support regarding substance use and abuse within healthcare settings. It also revealed serious inadequacies within the nursing profession for identifying, intervening, and supporting nurses with substance use disorders. The following recommendations are for nurse administrators, educators, and healthcare agencies intended to assist individuals entering the nursing profession, support those who are silently suffering with a substance use disorder within the profession and provide the necessary protection for patients being treated by nurses who have this disorder and are actively using and abusing drugs and or alcohol.

Increase Training in Nursing Schools About Substance Use Disorders

There needs to be a greater content emphasis on substance abuse and addiction for nurses and other health professionals in nursing schools. Recognition of the role that family history of alcohol and drug use plays in a predilection for abuse needs to be heightened. Those with a family history need to be informed of their susceptibility to addiction. Nursing schools should require extensive education about the dangers of prescription medications and self-medicating and the damage engaging in addictive behavior does to the nurse, patients, and the hospital environment. These trainings should have periodic refresher courses.

Teach Nurses the Importance of Good Self-Care and Acceptable Coping Skills

This study corroborates that nurses, as frontline healthcare professionals, are in high stress positions, yet there are no support systems to help them cope with and respond to the stresses of the role. To remain healthy, good self-care and coping skills are essential for nurses who are practicing in stressful working conditions. Nursing schools and healthcare settings need to incorporate mindfulness training and other formal methods for stress management into their training programs.

Periodic Training Updates for Managers and Supervisors Related to Identifying, Intervening, and Supporting Nurses with Substance Use Disorders

There are specific signs and symptoms that occur to alert coworkers, supervisors, and managers regarding drug diversion and drug use by colleagues. Training should be provided regarding policies within the healthcare setting related to this behavior. Managers and supervisors should be well trained on how to identify, confront, and support the substance abuser. They should be aware of the resources available for these nurses and of their vulnerabilities, the issues surrounding drug addiction, and the dangers it poses to both the nurse and the nurse's patients and the hospital environment.

Random Drug Screens in Nursing Schools and at the Workplace

Based on the findings from this study, there is an apparent need to conduct random drug screens in nursing schools and hospitals, clinics, or wherever controlled substances or substances of abuse are available. These drug screens should include testing for the opiates/drugs in the units where nurses who are screened are working. Although this may require legislation, it is important to understand the value this would have, not only as it relates to public protection, but also as it relates to early identification of nurses who are using and abusing substances.

Mandatory Reporting

Mandatory reporting is a policy that should be adopted by all states regarding criminal activity by any nurse or nursing student. As a matter of public protection and protection for the nurse, mandatory reporting to the appropriate nursing regulatory agency by supervisors and managers will prevent a nurse who is fired from one healthcare center for diverting or abusing substances to just move to the next institution and continue their addictive behavior, thereby endangering new patients and allowing the nurse to go longer and deeper into his or her disease.

Develop A "Place of Safety" Within Healthcare Institutions

There needs to be a "place of safety" within hospitals and other healthcare institutions where nurses who are stressed and facing personal and professional difficulties can confidentially go for support. Polices and processes need to be developed within hospitals and other healthcare institutions to provide resources and personal and professional help, understanding, and care for nurses.

RECOMMENDATIONS FOR FUTURE RESEARCH

As a result of the growing problem of prescription drug abuse and legalizations of marijuana across the country, for public protection and safety, further research needs to be conducted to determine the impact these changes may be having on the nursing profession.

The following are recommendations for further research:

1. Replicate this study and increase the involvement of men and those from other ethnicities and broader geographic settings to validate these findings. The voices of additional nurses may offer greater understanding of the complexity of substance use disorders and the importance of recovery support systems in the nursing profession.
2. Conduct a meta-analysis of nursing school programs to identify best practice and share curricula on substance use and abuse education.
3. Conduct a study with nursing supervisors and administrators to recognize the issues they face in confronting drug use and abuse.

Substance use and abuse in nursing is an extremely complex phenomenon. It causes loss and impacts nurses' personal and professional lives and patient care. Family history and early drug use are major risk factors for nurses developing substance use disorders early in life. The use of alcohol and substances may begin before or in nursing school. Yet, there is minimal education and training regarding substance abuse in healthcare settings, and the participants had little insight about the disease and their own personal risk factors.

Throughout the study, rich, thick, descriptive examples of how each participant's life was impacted by the disease and how some type of crisis, confrontation, or major event led to a "wake up call," a jolt and moment of reckoning are offered. These experiences evidence how the participants were able to transform from an addiction lifestyle to a recovery lifestyle, accomplished only with the support of others. Generally, that support did not come from their healthcare settings, but from outside sources. It took support, resources, and help from the larger recovery community for these nurses to face their addiction and to continue across years of recovery to stay drug and alcohol free.

There is a major change that happens when an addicted nurse finds recovery. That nurse gains an entirely new lifestyle. The nurse is transformed from a life that was filled with deception, shame, and despair to a new existence filled with hope and gratitude. The participants traveled from that of great loss, humiliation, and secrecy surrounded by tragedy and depravation to lives full of love, support, and purpose.

> The fact of the matter is that we do have a responsibility to lead clean and sober lives if we're going to be in this profession, taking care of patients and people's loved ones. There is an expectation that we will be clear minded at work. And do the best we can, and I didn't get that before! (Purple Lilly)

Index

About the Author

Dr. Carol Stanford is an adjunct professor at William Jessup University and has been a part of the nursing community for over 25 years. She has formulated policies as necessary; identified and implemented best practices and effective innovations to monitor RNs in recovery. She has provided expert testimony, developed guidelines, protocols, procedural manuals, program videos and brochures related to nursing and addiction. She has provided education and conducted training related to substance use disorders at universities, hospitals, and doctor and nursing conferences across the United States. She was a participating author of the National Council State Boards of Nursing resource manual, *Substance Use Disorder in Nursing,* developed for nursing boards across the country. She has a passion for supporting public health and the nursing population which is a vital part of the healthcare community.

www.ingramcontent.com/pod-product-compliance
Lightning Source LLC
Chambersburg PA
CBHW021820270326
41932CB00007B/266